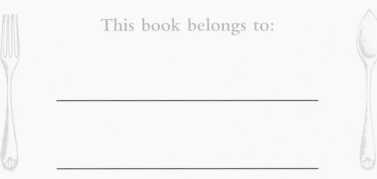

This book belongs to:

_____

_____

Rose Marie Donhauser

Apples & Pears

Favorite Recipes

Design: Heidrun Schröder, Christiane Leesker
Production: Patty Holden
Translator: Christie Tam
Editors: Monika Römer, Lisa M. Tooker, Ann Beman
Published originally under the title Äpfel & Birnen Lieblingsrezepte ©2002 Verlag W. Hölker
GmbH, Münster. English translation for the U.S. market ©2004 Silverback Books, Inc.

ISBN: 1-930603-93-2

Printed in China

CONTENTS

Unless otherwise indicated, all recipes make four servings.

PREFACE

First the bad news: This book isn't big enough to hold all my countless recipes, inspirations, and ideas on what to do with apples and pears. To fit everything in, the book would have to be at least twice as thick.

Now for the good news: I chose my best, favorite, and most fantastic recipes, retested them and re-tasted them. And as a result of all this cooking, I got totally carried away inventing new apple and pear combinations! And the only way I could include my absolute favorite recipe—a quick and easy Apple Curry—was to insert it in the preface, since there just wasn't any room anywhere else. But that's alright because not every recipe holds this honor.

And so—I heat vegetable oil in a wok and stir-fry three onions cut into strips, along with two apples cut into small slices. I then stir in a little green Thai curry paste, dust everything with curry powder, and pour in a little stock or white wine, and one can of coconut milk. Then I add strips of one chicken breast and cook them gently until tender. I check the refrigerator to see if I can find a few pea eggplants, some oyster mushrooms, and a stalk of lemon grass. If not, that's fine. If so, there is much rejoicing. I clean them, dice them finely, and add them to the curry. I take a taste to find out if it needs a little salt and pepper, then I round it all off with a shot of Thai fish sauce, if I have any—but it also works without. I accidentally spill a spoonful of steaming curry onto my Preface and figure I must have written enough by now, and have probably managed to whet your appetite for curry, apples, pears, and the whole cookbook. Oh, and by the way, try this Apple Curry with aromatic Thai rice or regular basmati rice and I promise this cookbook will be one that you won't soon forget!

Bon appetit and culinary greetings from your apple pear author,

INTRODUCTION

Cultivated apples and pears are classified generally as "pome fruit," along with quinces and several types of wild fruit, including rosehips and hawthorn. As indicated in the preface, the two most important representatives of this group— apples and pears— are already so interesting from both a botanical and a culinary point of view that they provide more than enough material for an entire cookbook.

The Apple—From Paradise to the Present

The apple is the central Christian symbol representing our exile from paradise. It is synonymous with the Fall of Man and is known as the fruit of the Tree of the Knowledge of Good and Evil. It also symbolizes love, luck, health, beauty, and power, all covered in detail in world literature. For instance, in his monumental novel *Cider House Rules*, John Irving not only created some wonderful characters but also paid homage to the Apple of Eden, which, although we tend to take it for granted, is a constant part of our lives.

Dr. Wilbur Larch, one of the novel's main characters, is a physician running an orphanage. Homer Wells is the only one of his young orphans always to be returned by his adoptive parents. As a young man, Homer meets Candy and Wally and leaves with this couple to work in their apple orchard. Larch, Homer's foster father, reluctantly lets him go. "And people will always eat apples, he thought— it must be a nice life." Homer not only learns all about apple harvesting but also gleans lessons about life.

From today's perspective, the first bite into the forbidden fruit that supposedly excluded us from paradise forever could not have been particularly tasty. History tells us it must have been a wild apple, an ancestor of our present-day cultivated apple. This is probably true, since many types of fruit and vegetable were not eaten until they had been properly cultivated, hybridized, and grown on a large scale.

Indeed, the wild apple of western Asia— more specifically, the region between the Black and Caspian Seas in the Caucasus— has had a long and complex history. About 5000 years ago, the Assyrians brought the first crabapples and paradise apples to Egypt. As a result of various wars, such as the campaign of Alexander the Great, apples continued their journey to Greece, Italy and, from there, to all the other European countries. The first apple tree didn't arrive in America until 1620, even though Columbus had already returned to Europe with the best and most beautiful foods from America 150 years earlier.

Cultivation, Harvesting, and Availability

The cultivated apple *(Malus domestica)* is a member of the rose family *(rosaceae)*. Following its domestication, many different varieties were developed from hybrids. The most important original forms are the common apple *(Malus pumila)*, European crabapple *(Malus dasyphylla)*, plumleaf crabapple *(Malus prunifolia)*, and common crabapple *(Malus sylvestris)*. There are over 20,000 kinds of apples worldwide, about 2,500 in the U.S. alone. Apple trees are no longer grown from seeds or cuttings, but by grafting a twig of a particular type onto a rootstock.

Over the past few years, many antique apple varieties have ceased to be available in stores, either due to marketing considerations or because they require too much care. Nevertheless, apple scientists (known as pomologists) have started taking precautions to prevent the extinction of endangered apple types by growing them in gardens or museums.

Apples grow best in temperate climates with a slightly elevated humidity, either in orchards or as individual trees. Apples can be grown on standard trees, half-standard trees, or espaliers. Depending on the type, they are harvested from July to January. Apple varieties are designated by the season of harvest, with a distinction being made between summer, fall, and winter apples. From 10 to 30 varieties are commonly available in markets, largely due to imports of apples from all over the world. In winter, fruit stands hold pretty arrangements of large, red-cheeked apples from New Zealand, green apples from the U.S., and yellow-red apples from Australia. Some local varieties can also be stored and made available throughout the year.

Nutritional Value

Today, the apple tree is the most widely cultivated of all fruit trees. The nutritional value of apples is one of the main reasons why they make up more than 80% of our total fruit harvests. The fact that "an apple a day keeps the doctor away" is clearly a tribute to its healthy ingredients. An apple contains about 3 oz of water, 12 g carbohydrate, 2.5 g fiber, and 0.28 g protein. In addition, they provide essential vitamins, including vitamin C, vitamin B1, vitamin B2, vitamin K, folic acid, and niacin.

Their carbohydrate content is mainly comprised of pectin, cellulose, and non-digestible fiber, which lowers cholesterol, regulates blood sugar levels, and promotes digestion. In this way, apples may help prevent diabetes and colon cancer.

Almost all the nutrients are directly under the skin, so it's recommended that you rinse the apple well and eat it with the peel still on. Apples are also a favorite because they're low in calories.

The Who's Who of Major Apple Varieties

- Belle de Boskoop: Winter apple, harvested from October–January. Fruity, slightly tart eating, baking, and cooking apple, stores well.
- Braeburn: Summer apple, harvested in Europe from May–September. Available year-round in New Zealand. Medium to large eating apple with an orangish-red blush over a green-yellow background; very firm, juicy, and sweet.
- Cortland: Winter apple, harvested from October to spring. Large red striped with purple; tart with soft texture; for eating, baking, and drying.
- Cox's Orange Pippin: Winter apple, harvested from October to mid-November. Tangy, yellowish-red eating, baking, and cooking apple.
- Empire: Fall apple, harvested from September–November. A crisp, snacking apple and is a cross between a Red Delicious and a McIntosh.
- Golden Delicious: Winter apple, harvested from October to January. Crisp and firm to slightly tender eating, baking, and cooking apple with a sweet aroma.
- Granny Smith: Winter apple, harvested from December–January. Light-green eating apple with firm, very juicy flesh.

- Gravenstein: Summer apple, harvested from August–September. Sweet-tart, yellow-green to reddish-yellow eating, baking, and cooking apple.
- Ida Red: Fall apple, harvested from October–November. Rich, sweet, medium-sized. Used for sauce, baking, and canning.
- Jonagold: Winter apple, harvested from late October to mid-December. Yellowish with a red blush, sweet, slightly tart eating, baking, and cooking apple. A cross between Jonathan and Golden Delicious. Stores well.
- Jonathan: Winter apple, harvested from October–December. Accidental result of mutants, slightly tart, sweet eating, baking, and cooking apple. Stores well.
- McIntosh: Fall apple, harvested September–October. Juicy two-toned red and green sauce, cider, and eating apple.
- Newtown Pippin: Fall apple, harvested September through October. Pale green to russet yellow tart pie and eating apple.
- Northern Spy: Fall apple, harvested October through early November. Pale green to yellow striped, red apple with spicy, sweet-tart flavor. Considered one of the best all-purpose apples.
- Red Delicious: Fall apple, harvested September–October. Brilliant red, popular eating apple.
- Rome Beauty: Winter apple, harvested October–June. Large and deep red baking, drying, and cider apple.
- Rubinette: Fall apple, harvested from September–December. Green with reddish stripes, eating, baking, and cooking apple with crisp, juicy sweet flesh. A cross between Golden Delicious and Lady Williams.
- Winesap: Fall apple, harvested October–November. Small deep red, tart and firm eating, sauce, and pie apple that stores well.

The Pear—"Gift of the Gods"

The quote above is from Homer's *Odyssey*. In his Greek homeland, pears were already being cultivated in sumptuous groves in the eighth century BC. They had traveled from Turkey to Greece via Persia, but were already in the form of cultivated pears developed from different wild varieties. The Romans didn't start cultivating pears until 1000 AD, when they first brought fruit cultivation across the Alps and into the northern regions. After apples, pears are the most widespread and well-known pome fruit in the world. Like apples, they are available year-round and are great favorites, but their worldwide production is only a third as large as that of the apple, mainly because they aren't as easy to store and are more complicated to process and prepare than apples.

Cultivation, Harvesting, and Availability

The pear *(Pyrus domestica)* is a member of the rose family *(rosaceae)*. Its most important ancestors include the common pear *(Pyrus communis)* and various wild varieties. By the 16th century, 50 different types of pear were already recognized in Germany. New varieties were passionately cultivated up until the 19th century, mainly in cloisters. Today there are more than 2,500 pear varieties worldwide, though only a fraction of these ever reach the markets. About 25 types are commonly available in Europe, Asia, and North Africa, while eight primary varieties are marketed in the U.S. New cultivated varieties continue to be developed in the Far East. In contrast to the less "sensitive" apples, pears did not become an important commercial fruit until after the development of cold storage. Nevertheless, summer and fall pears still need to be used as soon after harvesting as possible. As with apples, many pear varieties have been lost — because, for example, it was no longer profitable to grow them. The major producers in order of importance are: France, Italy, Germany, Austria, Holland, Belgium, Chile, Argentina, the United States, and South Africa.

A basic distinction is made between eating and cider pears, the latter playing only a very minor role on the pear market. In addition, pears are classified by the season of harvest as summer, fall, and winter pears.

Although very enjoyable when eaten, raw pears are even more interesting when further processed, whether cooked, canned, juiced, or used in alcoholic perry (pear cider). In combination with alcohol, pears are clearly superior to apples. The explanation is simple: Pears are much less acidic than apples, providing a smoother drinking experience when distilled into schnapps, brandy, and liqueurs. The crowning glory in a pear's career is to be processed into pear brandy.

Nutritional Value

Pears are especially useful in dietetic cooking because their low fruit acid content makes them easy to digest. They are rich in vitamins and minerals.

An average pear contains almost 3 oz water, 0.47 g protein, 0.29 g fat, 10 g carbohydrate, and 2.8 g fiber. In addition, they provide several milligrams of vitamin B1, vitamin B2 and niacin, and high amounts of vitamin C. However, the individual varieties sometimes deviate significantly from these average values. Pears are almost the same as apples, averaging about 55 calories each.

The Who's Who of Major Pear Varieties

- Bosc: Fall pear, harvested from October–November. Green, elongated eating pear with crisp, firm flesh and a mild aroma.
- Anjou: Winter pear, harvested from October through May. Large, russet-colored, egg-shaped pear good for eating and cooking. Stores well.
- Bartlett: Summer pear, harvested from mid-August to October. Green, very plump, juicy, sweet, and musky eating, cooking, and baking pear. This pear is known as the "Queen of Pears."
- Comice: Summer pear, harvested September–March. Rounded, chubby, and green, this pear is sweet, juicy, buttery, and perfect for dessert.
- Forelle: Summer pear, harvested September through March. Golden yellow with crimson flesh, this pear looks like a little Bartlett and is the perfect winter holiday pear.
- Nellis: Winter pear. Large and rounded, dark green cooking pear with spicy flavor, and buttery texture.
- Seckel: Winter pear, harvested September-Febuary. This tiny russet-skinned pear is excellent for eating and ideal for pickling and canning.

APPETIZERS AND
SMALL DISHES

Pear Boats with Herb Yogurt

2 pears, 5 tbs port wine, 16 slices Parma or Serrano ham,
For the herb yogurt: 3 fresh stalks oregano,
1 cup plain yogurt, Juice of ⅓ lemon, 1 tb olive oil,
Salt, Freshly ground black pepper

Peel pears, cut in half, core, and cut each half into 4 wedges. In a bowl, toss pear wedges with port wine and let marinate briefly.

In the meantime, prepare the herb yogurt: Rinse oregano and pat dry. Pluck leaves from stalks and cut into strips. Combine oregano, yogurt, lemon juice, and olive oil. Season with salt and pepper and transfer to 4 individual bowls.

Wrap 1 slice ham around each marinated pear wedge and arrange 4 wedges on each plate with a small bowl of dip.

☞ You don't have to marinate the pear wedges. You can also serve them plain and crisp, wrapped in a ham blanket.

Apple Carpaccio with Shaved Parmesan

2 apples, 7 oz whole Parmesan cheese, 4 tbs olive oil,
2 tbs balsamic vinegar, Salt, Freshly crushed black pepper,
2 tbs raisins and/or 2 tbs pine nuts (optional),
1 oven-fresh baguette

Peel apples, core with an apple corer, and cut into very fine rings with a kitchen slicer. Spread out apple rings decoratively on 4 plates. Cut Parmesan into fine shavings, using a special cheese slicer, vegetable slicer or vegetable peeler, and scatter over the apple rings.

Combine olive oil, balsamic vinegar, salt and pepper, and beat vigorously. Drizzle over plates, 1 tbs at a time. If desired, sprinkle with raisins and/or pine nuts. Cut baguette into thin slices and serve on the side.

Ham Rolls with Ricotta Apple Sauce

⅔ cup ricotta, 3½ tbs horseradish cream, 1 apple,
Salt, Freshly ground black pepper, 12 slices cooked ham

Combine ricotta and horseradish. Peel apple, cut in half, core, and grate finely on a kitchen grater. Stir into ricotta and season with salt and pepper.

Place individual ham slices on a work surface, spread with ricotta mixture, and roll up. Arrange 3 ham rolls on each appetizer plate.

☞ Serve with Italian-style mixed marinated vegetables and toasted white bread.

Puff Pastry Pockets with Fruit and Ham

⅔ lb frozen puff pastry dough, thawed (about 10½ oz)
For the filling: 3½ tbs celery root, 1 small apple, 1 small pear,
2 tbs butter, Salt, Freshly ground pepper,
½ tsp caraway seeds, ½ tsp dried marjoram,
3½ tbs pickled beets (canned), 3½ tbs cooked ham,
7 tbs herb crème fraîche (from gourmet shops or substitute herb sour cream)
Plus: Flour for the work surface, 3½ tbs melted butter,
1 egg yolk, Butter for the baking sheet

For the filling: Peel celery root, apple, and pear. Core apple and pear and finely dice apple, pear, and celery root. In a pan, heat butter and briefly braise diced ingredients. Season with salt, pepper, caraway, and marjoram. Drain beets and cut into strips. Cut ham into strips. Lightly toss beets with the contents of the pan and the herb crème fraîche.

One at a time, place puff pastry sheets on a floured work surface and divide into squares with edges about 4-inches long. Place 1 tbs filling in the center of each square, fold in the two sides, and roll up. Whisk butter and egg yolk, brush onto edges, and press together firmly.

Place pastry pockets on a buttered baking sheet and brush with butter-egg yolk mixture. In an oven preheated to 400°F, bake for about 20 minutes until golden and crispy. Remove and let cool for 10 minutes before serving.

☞ Goes with crème fraîche as a dip and sauerkraut enriched with cream.
☞ These pockets taste even better cold, making them ideal picnic food.

Pear Toast with Roquefort

4 slices whole-wheat bread, 2 tbs softened butter,
8 paper-thin slices of smoked ham, 1 large pear,
Juice of ¼ lemon, 7 oz sliced Roquefort cheese

Toast bread and spread with a little butter. Place smoked ham on top. Peel pear, cut into quarters, core, and cut into small slices. Drizzle with lemon juice and arrange on ham slices. Spread with remaining butter and top with Roquefort. Place toast on a baking sheet. Preheat oven to 400°F, set to broil, and heat under the broiler.

☞ Goes with butterhead lettuce dressed with vinaigrette.

Ham and Cheese Toast with Apples

4 slices white bread, 1 tbs softened butter, 4 slices cooked ham, 2 apples,
Juice of ½ lemon, 4 thick slices Emmenthaler cheese, 2 tbs cranberry sauce

Toast bread lightly and spread with a little butter. Place 1 slice of ham on each. Peel apples, cut into quarters, core, slice, and drizzle with lemon juice. Arrange apple slices on ham and brush with remaining butter. Top with cheese and place toast on a baking sheet. Preheat oven to 400°F, set to broil, and heat under the broiler. Before serving, top each slice with 1 dollop cranberry sauce.

☞ Delicious with sour cherry compote.

English Toast with Pears

1 pear, 7 tbs dry white wine, 1 tsp sugar,
4 slices white bread, 1 tsp butter, 4 slices cooked ham
For the cheese sauce: ⅔ lb Gloucester cheese (about 10½ oz),
5 tbs pale beer, 1 tbs hot mustard, 2 egg yolks,
Salt, Freshly ground white pepper

Peel pears, cut into quarters, and core. Combine wine, sugar, and 7 tbs water, bring to a boil and add pear pieces. As soon as the mixture starts to boil, switch to low heat and cook gently for 5 minutes. Toast bread slices, spread with butter, and top each with 1 slice of ham. Remove pear slices from saucepan, cut into fans, and spread out on bread slices.

For the cheese sauce: Grate cheese finely with a kitchen grater and combine with beer, mustard, and egg yolks. In a heat-resistant bowl, beat over a hot double boiler until thick and creamy. Season cheese mixture with salt and pepper and spoon onto toast. Place toast on a baking sheet. Preheat oven to 400°F, set to broil, and heat under the broiler for 5–8 minutes.

☞ You can also spread cheese toast with apple jelly, if you prefer (see recipe on page 106).

Sweet and Spicy Stock with Apple Wedges

1 cup meat stock, 1 small onion, 1 tart apple,
1 dash apple cider vinegar, 1 pinch sugar

Bring meat stock to a boil and then simmer gently over low heat. Peel onion, cut in half, then into strips, and stir into stock. Simmer for another 5 minutes. Peel apple, cut into quarters, core, and cut into thin wedges. Place apples in the stock and cook gently for 5–6 minutes. Season with apple cider vinegar and sugar. Serve in preheated soup bowls.

Smoked Eel in Vegetable Stock with Pears

1 small carrot, 7 tbs celery root, 1 green onion, Salt, 1 pear,
²⁄₃ cup dry white wine, 1 tbs sugar, 1 whole clove,
1¾ cups smoked eel cups (about 14 oz), 2 cups fish stock (canned)

Peel carrot and celery root and cut both into fine strips. Clean green onion, cut in half crosswise, and cut into fine strips. Place vegetable strips in boiling, salted water, briefly bring to a boil, pour into a colander, and rinse under cold water.

Peel pear, cut into quarters, and core. Combine white wine, sugar, and clove, bring to a boil and add pear wedges. As soon as the mixture starts to boil, switch to medium heat and cook gently for 3 minutes. Remove pear pieces, let cool, and cut into strips about ³⁄₈-inches wide. Skin smoked eel and cut into ³⁄₈-inch pieces.

Bring fish stock to a boil and add vegetable strips, eel, and pear just long enough to heat them. Serve in preheated cappuccino cups, small soup bowls, or decorative soup plates.

☞ The slightly sweet pear, smoky fish, and the spring vegetable aromas form a unique flavor combination. Best served at a stand-up buffet with champagne.

Crostini with Apple Chicken Livers

1 shallot, 1 apple, 1 cup chicken livers, 3 stalks parsley,
½ cup olive oil, 2 tbs sherry,
Salt, Freshly ground black pepper, 12 small bread slices

Peel and mince shallot. Peel apple, cut into quarters, core, and dice finely. Rinse chicken livers under cold running water, pat dry with paper towels, and chop very finely. Rinse parsley, pat dry, pluck off leaves, and chop finely.

In a pan, heat 6 tbs olive oil and briefly braise shallots and apple. Add chicken livers and sauté while stirring. Pour in sherry and cook for about 5 more minutes.

Remove pan from heat, stir in parsley, and season with salt and pepper. Brush bread slices with remaining olive oil. Preheat oven to 400°F, set to broil, and heat under the broiler until crispy. Remove, spread with warm apple chicken livers, and serve.

☞ You can also garnish crostini with parsley sprigs. Serve with cold cider (or apple wine).

Squash Apple Soup

2¼ lb squash (buttercup), 7 oz potatoes,
1 large tart apple (e.g., Granny Smith), 1 onion, 3 tbs butter,
1 cup chicken stock, 1 cup apple wine (or apple juice),
½ tsp curry powder, ½ tsp chili powder, Salt, Freshly ground pepper,
½ tsp balsamic vinegar, ½ cup heavy cream, 2 tbs pumpkin seeds

Peel squash, remove fibers and seeds, and dice flesh. Peel potatoes and dice. Peel apple, cut into quarters, core, and dice. Peel and dice onion.

In a large saucepan, melt butter and briefly braise diced squash, potatoes, apple, and onion. Pour in stock, bring to a boil, and cook for 15 minutes. Then add apple wine (or juice) and season with curry, chili powder, salt, and pepper. Purée soup, season to taste with balsamic vinegar, and enrich with cream. Toast pumpkin seeds in an ungreased pan and sprinkle over the hot soup.

Pear and Apple Muesli

The original muesli from Switzerland—created and named by Dr. Bircher-Benner—is a mixture (or "müesli" in Germany) made from cracked wheat, honey, fruits, seeds, and milk. Today, everybody makes muesli with their own favorite ingredients. Regardless of whether you use yogurt or seeds, the important thing is that it's healthy and provides you with a fortified breakfast for the day ahead.

Makes 2 servings
3½ tbs rolled oat flakes, 7 tbs apple juice, 2 tbs honey,
3½ tbs sliced almonds, 1 apple, 1 pear, 1 cup plain yogurt, 2 tbs raisins

Combine oats, apple juice and honey, and place in 2 large glass bowls. Sprinkle with sliced almonds. Peel apple and pear, cut into quarters, core, cut into wedges, and distribute over oatmeal. Stir yogurt and spoon onto fruit. Sprinkle with raisins and serve.

Griebenschmalz

1 lb raw pork fat without the skin,
1 stalk fresh marjoram, 1 small tart apple

Cut pork fat into cubes of about ¼ inch and render in a saucepan for about 45 minutes over low heat. The fat will become liquid and cracklings will form in the bottom of the pan. In the meantime, rinse marjoram, pat dry, pluck off leaves, and add. Peel apple, cut into quarters, core, and add to fat 20 minutes after you start rendering it.

When the fat is done, remove marjoram and apple pieces. Ladle fat and cracklings into small stoneware pots and let congeal in the refrigerator.

☞ Schmalz is a favorite spread for hearty farm bread, accompanied by beer or wine. If you want, you can also chop up the apple pieces and let them congeal in the fat.

SALADS AND VEGETABLE DISHES

Baked Sauerkraut Pear Salad on Hash Browns

*For the salad: 1 pear (e.g., Bosc), 3½ oz cooked, sliced ham,
1 cup sauerkraut (prepared product), 3 tbs heavy cream
For the hash browns: 1 lb firm potatoes,
Salt, Freshly ground black pepper, 3½ tbs clarified butter
Plus: ⅔ cup sliced blue cheese (e.g., Gorgonzola)*

Peel pear, cut into quarters, core, and cut into small slices. Cut ham into strips. In a saucepan, heat sauerkraut and cream. Add pear and ham. As soon as the mixture starts to boil, remove from heat.

For the hash browns: Peel potatoes and grate finely with a kitchen grater. Firmly squeeze out potatoes to extract liquid and season with salt and pepper.

In 1 large pan or 2 small ones, heat clarified butter. Use a tablespoon to transfer small mounds of potato to the hot fat, press them flat with the back of the spoon, brown, and turn. Place the golden brown and crispy mini-hash browns on a baking sheet. Top with the sauerkraut mixture and cheese slices and heat in an oven preheated to 400°F for about 10 minutes.

☞ If you're in a hurry, you can use frozen hash browns from your grocer's freezer.

Swedish Mimosa Salad

2 eggs, 2 beefsteak tomatoes, 1 ripe baby pineapple,
1 orange, 1 small cucumber, 1 apple, 1 pear, 7 oz sour cream,
7 tbs mayonnaise, Salt, Freshly ground white pepper

Place eggs in boiling water and boil for 10 minutes. In the meantime, blanch tomatoes, peel, remove seeds and core, and chop flesh into pieces of about ⅜ inch. Rinse eggs under cold water, peel, cut in half, and separate yolks from whites. Finely dice egg whites. Peel baby pineapple, cut into quarters lengthwise, remove core, and cut into small cubes. Peel orange, including the white membrane. Cut out segments from between the inner membranes and squeeze juice from discarded membranes. Peel cucumber, cut in half lengthwise, remove seeds, and slice. Peel apple and pear, core, and cut into small, thin slices. Combine sour cream, mayonnaise, and orange juice. Toss all salad ingredients lightly with the dressing and season with salt and pepper. Mash egg yolks with a fork and sprinkle over salad.

Pineapple Apple Salad with Onions

7 tbs grated coconut, 1 ripe baby pineapple, 2 onions,
3 stalks cilantro, 2 apples, Juice of 1 orange, 7 tbs sour cream,
Salt, Freshly ground black pepper,
½ tsp mild curry powder, 1 pinch cayenne pepper

In a hot, ungreased pan, lightly toast grated coconut while stirring. Transfer to a plate to cool. Peel baby pineapple, cut into quarters lengthwise, remove core, and cut into thin pieces. Peel onions, cut in half, and then into fine strips. Rinse cilantro, pat dry, pluck off leaves, and chop finely. Peel apples, cut into quarters, core, and cut into small slices. Mix these prepared ingredients with orange juice and sour cream. Season liberally with salt, pepper, curry, and cayenne. Cover salad and refrigerate for at least 1 hour. Just before serving, sprinkle with toasted grated coconut.

☞ Goes with grilled fish or barbecued steaks. This salad is ideal for a summer party.

Warm Lettuce Salad with Pears

For the salad: 2 butterhead lettuce hearts, Salt,
1 onion, 1 clove garlic, 7 oz heavy cream,
3½ tbs herb crème fraîche (from gourmet shops or substitute herb sour
cream), Freshly ground black pepper, 1 dash ground nutmeg
For garnish: 1 pear, 2 tbs butter, 1 tsp sugar, 2 tbs chopped walnuts

For the salad: Clean lettuce hearts, rinse, spin dry, and cut crosswise into strips. Blanch in boiling, salted water, rinse under cold water, and drain. Peel onion and garlic and mince. Bring cream to a boil, add minced onion and garlic, and simmer for 5 minutes.

In the meantime, prepare garnish: Peel pear, cut into quarters, core, and slice. In a pan, heat butter, stir in sugar, and caramelize. Swirl pear pieces and walnuts around in the butter.

Reduce heat under the onion-garlic cream, stir in crème fraîche and fold in lettuce strips. Remove pan from heat and season salad with salt, pepper, and nutmeg. Arrange on salad plates and top with the caramelized walnut-pear mixture.

☞ This salad is excellent as an appetizer with a mixed cold cut platter or at the end of a meal with a cheese platter. You can also serve it with hearty dark bread.

Radicchio with Pine Nuts and Pears

*3½ tbs pine nuts, 2 medium heads radicchio, 1 clove garlic, 1 shallot,
1 tsp hot mustard, 7 tbs olive oil, 2 tbs white balsamic vinegar,
Salt, Freshly ground black pepper, 1 pear*

In a hot, ungreased pan, toast pine nuts lightly while stirring. Remove and transfer to a plate to cool.

Clean radicchio, detach leaves, rinse, and spin dry. Peel garlic and shallot and mince, then combine with mustard, olive oil and balsamic vinegar, and beat vigorously. Season with salt and pepper.

Decoratively arrange radicchio leaves in rosettes on 4 plates. Peel pear, cut into quarters, core, and grate coarsely over the lettuce using a kitchen grater. Thoroughly whisk salad dressing once more and spoon onto the salad. Finally, sprinkle with toasted pine nuts.

☞ A very appetizing salad with a delicious flavor.

Fruity Cheese Salad

Try combining cheese and apple jelly for a nice, delicate flavor.

*1 cup sliced Emmenthaler cheese,
5½ oz smoked pork sausage (e.g., Kassler),
½ cup small purple and white grapes, 1 apple, 1 pear,
Juice of ½ orange, ⅔ cup plain yogurt, 1 pinch sugar,
1 tbs freshly chopped dill, Salt, Freshly ground black pepper
For garnish: ½ red bell pepper, 4 slices white bread, 1 tbs butter,
2 tbs apple jelly (see recipe on page 106)*

Cut cheese into narrow strips and thinly slice sausage. Rinse grapes, remove seeds, and pat dry with paper towels. Peel apple and pear, cut into quarters, core, and cut into small, thin slices. Combine these prepared ingredients in a bowl.

Make the dressing by mixing orange juice, yogurt, sugar, dill, salt, and pepper; pour over the salad and toss lightly.

For the garnish: Clean bell pepper, remove seeds and interior, and grate finely on a kitchen grater. Sprinkle lightly over the salad. Toast bread, and spread with butter and apple jelly. Transfer salad to 4 plates. Cut toast in half diagonally and arrange 2 halves on each salad plate.

Cauliflower Pear Salad

*1 small cauliflower, Salt, 2 small pears, 7 oz sour cream,
Juice of ½ lemon, 1 pinch sugar, Freshly ground black pepper
For garnish: 1 pinch cayenne pepper, 2 tbs sliced hazelnuts,
1 small pkg cress*

Clean cauliflower, cut into florets, and blanch in salted water. Pour into a colander, rinse under cold water, and let drain thoroughly. Peel pears, cut into quarters, core, and cut into small slices.

Combine sour cream, lemon juice, sugar, salt, and pepper. In a bowl, lightly toss dressing with cauliflower florets and pear slices. Transfer salad to 4 plates, dust with cayenne, and sprinkle with hazelnuts. Trim cress, rinse, pat dry, and distribute over the salad plates.

☞ Prepackaged taco shells are perfect for presenting salad on a plate and are highly recommended as a complementary "starch."

Waldorf-Astoria Salad

The salad described here is the original from the famous hotel, whereas the salad on the next page is a later vegetarian version. John Jacob Astor (1763–1848), who came from the village of Waldorf near Heidelberg in Germany, accumulated a fortune through various trades, including furs. He established his headquarters in Astoria, Oregon, which he made into a prospering town. With the fortune he accumulated, his great-grandson built a luxury hotel in New York and named it the Waldorf-Astoria. Of course, it wasn't Mr. Astor who invented the salad, but the maitre d'.

1 lb freshly cooked chicken, skinned and deboned,
1 orange, 7 tbs celery root, 1 apple, 2/3 cup mayonnaise,
4 tsp Madeira, 3 1/2 tbs chopped walnuts,
Salt, Freshly ground white pepper
For garnish: 4 nice butterhead lettuce leaves,
8 walnut halves

Cut chicken into fine strips. Peel orange, including the white membrane. Cut out segments from between the inner membranes. Squeeze juice from the discarded membranes and set aside. Peel celery root and apple. Cut apple into quarters, core, and cut both apple and celery root into thin strips. Combine mayonnaise, orange juice, and Madeira. Toss lightly with prepared salad ingredients and season liberally with salt and pepper.

Rinse lettuce leaves, spin dry, and lay flat on 4 appetizer plates. Arrange salad on top and garnish each with 2 walnut halves.

Waldorf Salad

In contrast to the original on the last page, this is a vegetarian version that has come to be known by the same name.

7 oz celery root, 2 apples, Juice of 1 lemon, ²⁄₃ cup mayonnaise,
3½ tbs chopped walnuts, Salt, Freshly ground white pepper
For garnish: 1 butterhead lettuce heart, 8 walnut halves

Clean celery root and cut into fine strips. Peel apples, cut into quarters, core, and cut into thin matchsticks. Lightly toss celery root, apples, and lemon juice. Add mayonnaise and walnuts and season with salt and pepper.

For the garnish: Clean lettuce heart, detach leaves, rinse, spin dry, and distribute on 4 plates. Arrange salad on top and garnish each with 2 walnut halves.

☞ Delicious with a baguette or walnut bread.

Pasta Salad with Apples and Pears

⅔ lb rigatoni (about 10½ oz), Salt, 3 beefsteak tomatoes,
⅔ cup mushrooms, 4 green onions, 1 apple, 1 pear,
Juice of ½ lemon, 1 clove garlic, 1 tsp medium-hot mustard,
1 egg yolk, 3½ tbs olive oil, 2 tbs sherry vinegar,
Freshly ground black pepper, 7 tbs freshly shaved Parmesan cheese

Cook pasta in a large amount of boiling, salted water for about 10 minutes until al dente. In the meantime, blanch tomatoes, rinse under cold water, peel, remove seeds and core, and cut into strips. Pour pasta into a colander, rinse under cold water, and drain.

Wipe mushrooms with a damp cloth and cut into very fine slices. Clean green onions, remove greens, and cut white parts into strips. Peel apple and pear, cut into quarters, core, cut into uniform bite-sized pieces, and drizzle with lemon juice. Peel and mince garlic.

Combine garlic, mustard, and egg yolk. Gradually add olive oil, then add vinegar, salt and pepper, and beat into a creamy dressing. Lightly toss all salad ingredients with the dressing and transfer to plates. Sprinkle with Parmesan.

☞ Instead of rigatoni, you can also use farfalle or elbow macaroni.
☞ Serve this nutritious salad with walnut bread or crispy tomato crostini taken straight out of the oven.
☞ To shave the Parmesan, just use a vegetable peeler.

Middle-Eastern Zucchini Salad

1 lb red onions, 1 lb zucchini, 7 tbs olive oil, 1 lb apples,
1 tsp coriander seeds, Juice of 1 lemon, 2 tbs white vinegar,
2 tbs brown sugar, ¼ tsp cinnamon, Salt, Freshly ground black pepper,
3½ tbs raisins, Juice of ½ orange, 3½ tbs pine nuts

Peel onions, cut in half, and then into strips. Clean zucchini, cut lengthwise into thin slices, and then crosswise into thin strips. In a large pan, heat olive oil and braise onion strips for 5 minutes. Add zucchini strips, stir well, and braise over low heat for another 8 minutes.

In the meantime, peel apples, cut into quarters, core, and slice. Crush coriander seeds coarsely in a mortar and add apple slices and coriander to the pan.

Season onion-zucchini mixture with lemon juice, vinegar, sugar, cinnamon, salt, and pepper. Pour into a bowl, cover, and refrigerate for 1 hour.

In the meantime, combine raisins and orange juice. In a hot, ungreased pan, toast pine nuts for 2 minutes while stirring. Let cool and chop coarsely.

Add orange raisins and pine nuts to salad. Add more seasoning to taste and serve.

☞ Delicious with oven-fresh flatbread.

Potato Salad with Apples and Roast Beef

1²⁄₃ lb potatoes, Salt, 1 onion, 3½ oz sliced roast beef, 1 cucumber,
4 tbs vegetable oil, 7 tbs meat stock, 2 tbs white wine vinegar,
2 small tart apples, 3½ tbs mayonnaise, 1 tsp hot mustard,
Freshly ground black pepper

Rinse potatoes and cook in boiling, salted water until done. Drain and let cool. In the meantime, peel and mince onion. Cut roast beef and cucumber into strips.

In a pan, heat 2 tbs vegetable oil and braise minced onion until translucent. Add meat stock, bring to a boil, and remove from heat. Peel and slice potatoes. In a bowl, combine remaining oil, white wine vinegar, roast beef and cucumber, and pour pan contents over the top. Peel apples, cut into quarters, core, and cut into small slices. Add apples, mayonnaise, and mustard to potato salad and stir. Season with salt and pepper.

☞ This potato salad tastes best when warm.

Beets and Apples with Rib Steak

1 lb beets, Salt, 1 tbs caraway seeds, 2 apples,
1 tsp sugar, 3 stalks parsley, 1 shallot, 6 tbs olive oil,
2 tbs red wine vinegar, ½ tsp hot mustard, Freshly ground black pepper,
2 rib steaks (about 7 oz each), 3 tbs vegetable oil

Scrub beets thoroughly under cold running water without damaging the skin. Place beets and caraway seeds in boiling, salted water, and cook over medium heat for up to 1 hour until done. Drain, rinse under cold water, peel, and slice thinly. Peel apples and core with an apple corer. Place in boiling water to which sugar has been added and return to a boil, then remove from water and cut into thin rings. Alternately arrange beet slices and apple rings in an overlapping pattern on 4 large plates.

Rinse parsley, pat dry, pinch leaves from stalks, and chop finely. Peel and mince shallot. Combine olive oil, vinegar, parsley, minced shallot, mustard, salt and pepper, and beat vigorously. Drizzle over beets and apples.

Season steaks with salt and pepper, and sear on both sides in hot vegetable oil. Fry over medium heat to the desired degree of doneness. Remove, cut into thin strips, and arrange steaks with meat juice next to the beets and apples.

☞ Serve this appetizing and nutritious "meat salad" with a baguette or whole-wheat bread.

Chicken Salad with Curry Dressing

Salt, 4 peppercorns, 3½ tbs dry white wine,
½ lb chicken breast fillet, 3½ oz fresh mushrooms,
2 tbs walnut halves, 3½ oz corn (canned),
3½ tbs mayonnaise, 3½ tbs sour cream, ¼ tsp curry powder,
Freshly ground black pepper, 1 apple

In a small saucepan, combine 2 cups water, salt, peppercorns and white wine, and bring to a boil. Add chicken breast, return to a boil, and simmer over low heat for 10 minutes. Remove pan from heat and leave meat in the stock for another 10 minutes. Remove, let cool, and cut into fine strips.

Wipe mushrooms with a damp cloth and, depending on their size, cut into halves or quarters. Chop walnuts coarsely and drain corn. Combine mayonnaise, sour cream, curry, salt, and pepper. Peel apple, core, grate finely with a grater, and stir into salad dressing. Lightly toss all ingredients and serve immediately.

☞ You can also make this salad with grilled chicken meat or cooked chicken breast from the deli.

Chicory with Apple Mustard Matjes Herring

2 eggs, 2 beefsteak tomatoes, 2 green onions, 2 heads chicory,
2 small tart apples, 4 Matjes herring fillets,
7 oz sour cream, 1 tb hot mustard, ¼ tsp curry powder,
Salt, Freshly ground black pepper, Juice of ¼ lemon, 1 bunch watercress
Plus: 8 paper-thin slices Parma ham, 8 grissini (thin, Italian breadsticks)

Boil eggs for 10 minutes. In the meantime, blanch tomatoes, peel, remove seeds and cores, and cut into strips. Clean and mince green onions.

Rinse eggs under cold water, peel, and chop finely. Clean chicory, cutting out the bitter core in a wedge and cutting off ⅜ inch of the root end. Cut leaves into strips and rinse. Peel apples, cut into quarters, core, and cut into matchsticks. Cut herring fillets into strips as fine as possible. Season sour cream liberally with mustard, curry, salt, pepper, and lemon juice.

In a bowl, lightly toss all prepared ingredients with the dressing and transfer to 4 plates. Trim watercress, rinse, shake dry, and scatter over salad. Wrap a ham slice around each grissini and garnish each salad plate with 2 breadsticks.

Raw Vegetables with Devil Sauce

1 zucchini, 1 carrot, 1 green bell pepper,
1 small kohlrabi (e.g., cabbage turnip), 2 apples, Juice of ½ orange
For the dip: 7 tbs mayonnaise, 7 tbs sour cream, 2 tbs tomato ketchup,
1 tsp brandy, 1 tsp lemon juice, A little Worcestershire sauce,
A few drops Tabasco, Salt, Freshly ground black pepper,
A touch of cayenne pepper

For the dip: Combine mayonnaise, sour cream, ketchup, brandy, and lemon juice. Season liberally with Worcestershire sauce, Tabasco, salt, and black pepper. Distribute sauce in 4 individual bowls and sprinkle with cayenne.

For the raw vegetables: Clean vegetables. Cut zucchini, carrot, bell pepper, and kohlrabi into uniform sticks. Arrange on 4 plates, separated by type, and place a bowl of dip in the center of each. Peel apples, cut into quarters, core, and cut into wedges. "Bathe" in a bowl of orange juice and arrange decoratively on the plates.

Shrimp Salad with Apples

2 tbs raisins, 2 tbs orange juice, 2 small tart apples,
3½ oz pineapple chunks with a little juice (canned), 7 oz peeled shrimp,
⅔ cup plain yogurt, Salt, Freshly ground black pepper, 1 pinch sugar,
1 pinch cayenne pepper, 2 butterhead lettuce hearts, 1 small onion,
2 tbs olive oil, 1 tbs sherry vinegar, 2 tbs slivered almonds

In a bowl, combine raisins and orange juice. Peel apples, cut into quarters, core, and cut into small slices. Stir pineapple chunks, shrimp, and yogurt into the raisin-juice mixture. Season with salt, pepper, sugar, and cayenne. Cover and let stand for about 10 minutes.

In the meantime, pull apart lettuce hearts, rinse, and spin dry. Peel onion, mince, and combine with olive oil, sherry vinegar, salt, and pepper. Immerse lettuce leaves in the dressing and arrange on 4 plates. Top with shrimp salad and sprinkle with slivered almonds.

HEARTY ENTRÉES
AND SIDES

Heaven and Earth

This dish, originating in the kitchens of the Rhineland, has a very symbolic name. Apples grow high in trees, thus representing heaven. Potatoes grow in the dirt and symbolize the earth. In times of want, this dish was a sort of culinary affirmation. No matter how bad things got, apples and potatoes were still available.

1²/₃ lb floury potatoes, Salt, 1 bay leaf, 1²/₃ lb tart apples,
²/₃ cup smoked bacon, 1 onion, A little grated peel of 1 lemon,
1½ tbs sugar, 1 tbs clarified butter, 3½ tbs softened butter

Rinse potatoes, peel, and cook in salted water with bay leaf for about 30 minutes until done. In the meantime, peel apples, cut into quarters, core, and cut into wedges. Finely dice smoked bacon. Peel and mince onion.

In a saucepan, combine apples, 7 oz water, lemon peel, and sugar and bring to a boil. Then simmer over low heat for 5–8 minutes until done. Heat clarified butter and fry diced bacon and minced onion for about 10 minutes until golden brown.

Drain potatoes, let cool enough to handle, and put through a ricer. Add butter and salt and stir. Partially drain apples and fold into mashed potatoes. Transfer to 4 plates and spoon bacon-onion mixture over the top.

☞ Goes with blood sausage, liverwurst, or cured ham.

Gorgonzola Fondue

For dipping: 1 baguette, 7 oz purple and white grapes, 2 pears,
2 apples, 3½ oz black and green olives
For the fondue: 14 oz Gorgonzola cheese (about 1¾ cups),
7 oz Géramont cheese (gourmet or cheese shops), 2 tbs cornstarch,
2 tbs Marsala (Italian dessert wine), 1 cup dry white wine

Cut baguette into uniform bite-sized pieces and place in a bread basket, wrapped in a cloth napkin. Rinse grapes, remove from stems, and pat dry with paper towels. Peel pears and apples, cut into quarters, core, and cut into pieces slightly smaller than the bread pieces. Transfer all dipping ingredients, including olives, to small bowls and place on the table.

Chop Gorgonzola and Géramont coarsely and combine in a saucepan with corn-starch, Marsala, and white wine. Melt cheese mixture over low heat while stirring with a wooden spoon until thick and creamy, pour into a fondue pot, and place on top of an alcohol burner on the table. Alternate dipping various ingredients in the cheese fondue.

☞ Serve fondue with a cold cut platter.
☞ The original fondue pot cannot be heated on the stove. However, cheese fondue pots are now available that are suitable for the stovetop and can then be set on an electrically heated base directly on the table.

Cheese Fondue with Fruits and Ham

For dipping: 1 baguette, ⅔ cup sliced cooked ham, 2 pears, 2 apples
For the fondue: 1 clove garlic, ⅔ lb Emmenthaler cheese (about 10½ oz),
⅔ lb Appenzeller cheese (about 10½ oz; gourmet or cheese shop),
1 tbs cornstarch, 1 cup cider (apple wine)
Plus: Coarsely cracked black pepper

Cut baguette into uniform bite-sized pieces and place in a bread basket, wrapped in a cloth napkin. Cut ham slices into pieces of about ¾ inch. Peel pears and apples, cut into quarters, core, and cut into bite-sized pieces. Transfer all dipping ingredients to separate serving bowls and place on the table.

For the fondue: Peel garlic, cut in half, and rub cut sides around the inside of a fondue pot. Using a kitchen grater, finely grate both types of cheese. In a saucepan, combine cheese, cornstarch and cider, and melt on the stove over moderate heat. Pour gently bubbling cheese mixture into a fondue pot and place on top of an alcohol burner on the table.

Thread a piece of ham and a piece of apple or pear onto a skewer and dip into the cheese fondue. Alternately dip bread and season each cheesy morsel with coarsely cracked black pepper.

Ramequin with Pears

*1 pear, 6 slices white bread, 6 slices cheese, ⅛ to ³⁄₁₆-inch thick Gruyère
or Emmenthaler cheese, 7 oz heavy cream, 2 eggs, Salt,
Freshly ground black pepper, 1 dash hot paprika, 2 tbs butter in bits
Plus: Butter for the casserole dish*

Peel pear, cut into quarters, core, and cut into small, thin slices. Cut bread and cheese slices in half. Butter a casserole dish and alternately arrange pear, bread, and cheese slices in an overlapping pattern in the bottom of the dish. Whisk cream and eggs, season with salt, pepper and paprika, and pour over the top. Place a few bits of butter on top. Bake in an oven preheated to 400°F for up to 30 minutes until golden brown and crispy.

☞ Goes with a green salad dressed with vinaigrette.

Potato Latkes with Spiced Apples

For the spiced apples: 3 apples (e.g., Granny Smith), ½ vanilla bean,
3½ tbs sugar, 1 cinnamon stick, 2 whole cloves, 2 star anise
For the latkes: 1 lb potatoes, 3 eggs, Salt, Freshly ground white pepper,
1 pinch grated nutmeg, About 7 tbs vegetable oil
Plus: 7 oz sour cream

For the spiced apples: Peel apples, core, and cut into wedges. In a saucepan, combine about ⅔ cup water, the pulp of the vanilla bean, sugar, cinnamon, cloves and star anise, and bring to a boil. Add apple wedges and as soon as it starts to boil, set aside for 10 minutes.

For the latkes: Rinse potatoes, peel, and grate finely with a kitchen grater. Combine potatoes and eggs and season with salt, pepper, and nutmeg. In a pan, heat vegetable oil, adding little by little as you fry the latkes. For each latke, place 1 tbs potato batter in the hot oil, flatten with the back of the spoon, fry until golden brown, turn, and finish frying.

Drain latkes on paper towels and place on preheated plates. Arrange spoonfuls of spiced apples around the latkes. Serve sour cream on the side or spoon onto top of each latke.

☞ A favorite Jewish dish.

Baked Grape and Ham Pears

½ cup sweet purple grapes, 2 pears, 8 slices cooked ham,
⅔ cup Parmesan cheese, ⅔ cup Stilton (English blue cheese), 2 tbs butter,
1 tbs flour, 1 cup milk, 7 oz heavy cream, 2 eggs
Plus: Butter for the casserole dish

Rinse grapes, remove stems, and pat dry with paper towels. Peel pears, cut into quarters, core, and cut into small slices. Cut ham slices into strips. Butter a casserole dish. Combine grapes, pears, and ham and distribute in the casserole dish.

Cut up Parmesan and Stilton. In a saucepan, heat butter until foamy and stir in flour. While stirring constantly, pour milk and cream into the roux. Bring to a boil and then reduce for another 5–8 minutes. Stir in both types of cheese, melt until smooth and creamy, and remove from heat. Let cheese sauce cool briefly. Separate eggs and stir egg yolks into sauce. Beat egg whites until stiff, fold in, and spread mixture evenly over the fruit-ham mixture. Bake in an oven preheated to 400°F for about 40 minutes until golden. Serve immediately.

Pear and Potato Gratin

1 lb potatoes, 2 pears, 1 tbs lemon juice, 4 tsp pear brandy (optional),
Salt, Coarsely crushed black pepper, 2 bay leaves, 1 cup heavy cream,
7 tbs freshly grated cheese (Gouda, Edam, or Emmenthaler)
Plus: Butter for the casserole dish

Rinse potatoes, peel, and slice thinly. Peel pears, cut into quarters, core, and slice. Alternately arrange potato and pear slices in an overlapping pattern in the bottom of a buttered casserole dish. Drizzle with lemon juice and brandy, if desired and season with salt and pepper. Place bay leaves on top and pour on cream. Cover casserole dish with aluminum foil and bake in an oven preheated to 350°F for about 30 minutes. Remove foil, sprinkle on the cheese, and heat under the broiler until golden.

Potato Pancakes with Apples and Yogurt Sauce

For the potato pancakes: 1 ⅔ lb potatoes, 1 small carrot,
2 apples, 2 tbs raisins, 2 tbs chopped hazelnuts,
7 tbs mixed rolled wheat and barley flakes, 2 eggs, 2 tbs sour cream
For the yogurt sauce: ½ bunch chives, 1 cup plain yogurt,
1 tsp lemon juice, Salt, Freshly ground black pepper
Plus: ¼ – ⅓ cup clarified butter for frying

For the potato pancakes: Rinse potatoes, peel, and grate finely with a kitchen grater. Firmly squeeze liquid out of potatoes. Peel carrot and apples and grate both with a kitchen grater. Combine potatoes, carrot, and apples with remaining potato pancake ingredients. Stir mixutre and let stand for about 10 minutes.

In the meantime, make the yogurt sauce: Rinse chives, pat dry, chop, and stir into yogurt. Season with lemon juice, salt, and pepper.

In a large pan, heat clarified butter, adding little by little as you fry the potato pancakes. For each pancake, place 1 tbs batter in the pan, flatten with the back of the spoon, fry until golden brown, and turn. Drain crispy pancakes on paper towels and serve with the yogurt sauce.

☞ These potato pancakes are known as "Datschi" in Bavaria, "Puffer" or "Püfferken" in Berlin, and in the Rhineland they're known as "Rievkooche." But all are basically the same thing: A basic batter of grated potatoes with various ingredients added, flattened in a pan, and fried.

Strudel with Pears and Blood Sausage

For the strudel dough: 7 oz flour, Salt,
7 tbs lukewarm water, 2 tbs vegetable oil
For the filling: 2 firm pears, 2 tbs sugar, 3 tbs pear brandy,
4 fresh blood sausages, 1 egg, Salt, Freshly ground black pepper,
½ tsp dried marjoram, A little grated peel of 1 lemon
For the sauce: 1 small onion, ⅔ cup cooked sauerkraut, 1 tbs butter,
17 oz gravy, Salt and freshly ground pepper as desired
Plus: Flour for the work surface, Butter for the baking sheet and for glazing

For the strudel dough: Sift flour and salt onto a work surface. With the back of your hand, make a well in the center and quickly work in water and oil. Knead into a smooth dough, wrap in plastic wrap, and set aside in a warm place for 30 minutes.

In the meantime, make the filling: Peel pears, cut into quarters, core, and slice. Combine pears, sugar, brandy and a shot of water, and braise until al dente. Squeeze blood sausage out of the casings, knead with egg until smooth, and season with salt, pepper, marjoram, and lemon peel. Roll out strudel dough on a floured kitchen towel. Distribute blood sausage mixture and pear slices on top, leaving a 2½–3 inch margin around the edges. Fold in the 2 sides and roll up the strudel. Slide it onto a greased baking sheet. Brush strudel liberally with butter and bake in an oven preheated to 400°F for about 35 minutes.

In the meantime, make the sauce: Peel and mince onion and chop sauerkraut. Briefly braise both in hot butter. Pour in gravy, bring to a boil, and season to taste with salt and pepper as needed. After baking, let strudel stand for about 15 minutes, slice, and serve with sauerkraut sauce.

Holstein Pear Dish with Green Beans

1²⁄₃ lb green beans, Salt, 1 cup smoked bacon, 1 onion,
½ bunch parsley, 2 fresh sprigs savory, Freshly ground black pepper,
1 cup meat stock, 4 firm pears

Clean beans and cut into thirds. Place in boiling, salted water and boil for 5 minutes. Pour into a colander, rinse under cold water, and drain. Dice bacon finely. Peel onion, cut in half, and then into strips. Rinse parsley, pat dry, pluck leaves from stalks, and chop finely. Rinse savory, but do nothing else.

In a large saucepan, render diced bacon and fry onion strips. Add beans, stir for several minutes, and season with salt and pepper. Add meat stock and as soon as it starts to boil, cover pan. Peel pears, cut into quarters, core, and add pears and savory to the pan. Let dish stew for 30 minutes.

☞ This dish, known as "Gröne Hein" (Green Heinrich), is a favorite in Holstein and is served with boiled potatoes.
☞ Instead of meat stock, you can use vegetable stock or water.

Boiled Potatoes with Apple-Onions and Pumpkin

2¼ lb potatoes, Salt, 1 tsp caraway seeds, 2 onions,
5 tbs vegetable oil, 2 apples, 2 tbs herb butter,
Salt, Freshly ground black pepper, 1 pinch sugar,
3½ tbs pumpkin seeds, ½ cup cream cheese, ½ cup cottage cheese,
1 tbs pumpkin seed oil (health food stores or gourmet markets)

Rinse potatoes. Boil potatoes and caraway seeds in salted water for about 30 minutes until done.

In the meantime, peel onions, cut in half, and then into strips. In a pan, heat oil and braise onion strips for about 5 minutes. Peel apples, cut into quarters, core, cut into wedges, and stir into the onions. Add herb butter and season with salt, pepper, and sugar. Continue braising over low heat for 5–8 minutes.

In a hot, ungreased pan, toast pumpkin seeds while stirring until they start to give off an aroma. Remove, let cool completely, and crush lightly in a mortar. Purée cream cheese and cottage cheese, then beat in pumpkin seed oil until mixture is thick and creamy.

Drain potatoes, let cool enough to handle, peel, and transfer to 4 plates. Arrange apple-onions next to the potatoes. Sprinkle pumpkin seeds onto pumpkin cream and serve on the side.

Fried Pears and Potatoes with Cheese

1 onion, 1⅔ lb potatoes boiled the day before, 2 pears,
3½ tbs clarified butter, Salt, Freshly ground black pepper,
7 oz blue cheese (Bavarian blue or Gorgonzola)

Peel onion and cut into strips. Peel potatoes and slice. Peel pears, core, and cut into thin wedges. In a large, ovenproof pan, heat clarified butter and briefly braise onion strips. Add potato slices and pear wedges and cook thoroughly for 10 minutes while stirring. Season with salt and pepper. Cut cheese into small pieces and sprinkle over the pan. Preheat oven to 350°F, set to broil, and slide pan under the broiler. Melt cheese for about 5 minutes and serve in the pan.

☞ Especially delicious with a large bowl of colorful, mixed salad.
☞ If you make fried potatoes from freshly boiled potatoes, they stick slightly to the bottom of the pan and don't become as crispy. It's best to follow the recipe and boil the potatoes the day before.

Roast Goose with Apple Chestnut Stuffing

Makes 8 servings
1 cleaned goose weighing about 11 lb
For the stuffing:, 1 lb chestnuts, 1 lb tart apples, Juice of 1 lemon,
2 tbs butter, Salt, 1 tbs sugar, 1 pinch dried marjoram, 7 tbs meat stock,
Freshly ground white pepper, 3 stalks fresh mugwort (pharmacy or
health food store), 7 oz boiling water, 5 oz pale beer
Plus: Metal or wooden skewers

For the stuffing: Using a small knife, cut an X into the surface of each chestnut. Place on a baking sheet and heat in an oven preheated to 400°F for about 20 minutes. In the meantime, peel apples, cut into quarters, and core. Then cut into small slices, place in a bowl, and drizzle with lemon juice.

Remove chestnuts from the oven, peel carefully, and cut in half. In a saucepan, heat butter and briefly braise chestnuts and apples while stirring. Season with salt, sugar and marjoram, and pour in stock. Braise over low heat for 3–4 minutes and remove from heat.

Wash goose thoroughly inside and out under cold running water. Rub dry with a kitchen towel and season inside and out with salt and pepper. Rinse mugwort sprigs and pat dry. Carefully stuff the goose cavity with mugwort and the apple-chestnut mixture. Close cavity with metal or wooden skewers (or sew shut with kitchen string). Place the goose in a roasting or broiler pan with the breast-side down and pour boiling water over the top. Place pan on the lowest rack of an oven preheated to 400°F. After roasting for about 1 hour, turn goose while piercing several times with a fork to help the goose fat escape. Occasionally baste goose with the fat.

After roasting for another 1½ hours, brush beer onto goose so it will form a nice crust. For the last 10 minutes, roast with the oven door open. Then take the goose out of the oven, cover it with aluminum foil, and let stand for 10 minutes. Strain meat juices into a saucepan and boil thoroughly for 10 minutes. Cut goose into about 8 pieces and arrange on a platter with the stuffing. Serve gravy separately.

☞ Excellent with Red Cabbage with Cinnamon Oranges and Apples (recipe on page 65).

☞ Goose gravy is always very rich. To remove fat from the gravy, lay a paper towel over the surface 2 or 3 times and discard it. If you want to remove even more fat, let the gravy cool and remove the congealed fat from the surface. In any case, a shot of apple schnapps will make the gravy easier to digest.

Blade Steaks in Pepper Apple Cream

1 large onion, 1 apple, 4 pork blade steaks,
Salt, Freshly ground white pepper, 3 tbs vegetable oil,
1 tbs butter, 3 tbs Calvados (apple brandy),
7 oz heavy cream, 2 tbs crushed green peppercorns

Peel onion, cut in half, and then into strips. Peel apple, cut into quarters, core, and cut into thin wedges.

Pound blade steaks slightly flat and season with salt and pepper. Fry in hot oil on both sides for 5 minutes. Transfer to a plate and cover with aluminum foil.

Add butter to meat juices and sauté onion strips and apple wedges for about 5 minutes. Pour in Calvados and add cream. Simmer gravy gently for 5–8 minutes. Stir in peppercorns and season with salt and pepper. Stir in meat juices from the steaks you set aside. Arrange steaks on plates and pour gravy over the top.

☞ You can also stir 1 tsp herbes de Provence into the sauce.

Sautéed Venison with Baked Apples

For the baked apples: 2 tbs raisins, 2 tbs rum, 4 ladyfingers,
1 tbs butter, 1 tbs sugar, 1 pinch cinnamon, 3½ tbs marzipan,
4 apples (e.g., Jonathan), ½ cup apple juice
For the venison: 1 lb shank of venison, 1 small onion,
⅔ cup mushrooms, 3 tbs vegetable oil, Salt, Freshly ground pepper,
1 tbs butter, 7 tbs game gravy (may use prepackaged gravy),
7 oz heavy cream
Plus: Butter for the casserole dish

For the baked apples: Pour rum over raisins. Crumble ladyfingers and sauté in hot butter for about 2 minutes. Stir in sugar, cinnamon, almond paste, and rum raisins. Rinse apples and remove about a ⅜-inch cap from the top of each. Then remove a wide margin of core using an apple corer. Fill apples with the marzipan mixture, replace caps, and place in a buttered casserole dish. Pour apple juice over the top and bake in an oven preheated to 350°F for about 30 minutes.

In the meantime, prepare the venison: Cut meat into fine strips. Peel and mince onion. Wipe mushrooms with a damp cloth, clean and, depending on their size, cut into halves or quarters.

In a pan, heat oil and briefly sauté venison strips on all sides in several batches. Transfer to a plate, season with salt and pepper, and cover with aluminum foil. Add butter to meat juices and briefly braise minced onion. Add mushrooms and continue sautéing and stirring until the mushroom liquid has boiled away. Add game gravy and cream and simmer gently for 5–8 minutes. Season to taste with salt and pepper and stir in meat strips, including juices. Place 1 baked apple in the center of each plate and spoon venison all around it.

☞ Serve with buttered noodles mixed with toasted almonds.

Venison Ragout with Red Wine Pears

2¼ lb venison shoulder
For the marinade: 3½ oz carrots, 3½ tbs celery root, ⅔ cup onions,
1 clove garlic, 8 juniper berries, 2 whole cloves, 10 peppercorns,
2 bay leaves, 1 sprig thyme, 1 qt dry red wine, 4 tbs vegetable oil,
Salt, Freshly ground pepper, 1 tbs tomato paste
For the red wine pears: 2 pears, 1 cup dry red wine,
Sugar, 4 tsp cranberry sauce

The day before cooking, remove membranes and sinews from venison and cut into 1¼-inch cubes. Coarsely dice carrots, celery root, and onions. Peel garlic and chop finely. Arrange meat cubes side by side in a broiler plan and top with chopped vegetables. Season with spices and herbs and pour on red wine. Cover with aluminum foil and marinate overnight.

On the next day, carefully pour marinade, including venison, through a strainer and save liquid. Remove meat and pat dry with paper towels.

In a large saucepan, heat vegetable oil and brown meat on all sides. Season with salt and pepper. Add drained vegetables and continue frying. Stir in tomato paste and brown. Add marinade and, if necessary, enough water to completely cover the meat and vegetables. Cover pan and stew over medium heat for 1 hour.

In the meantime, make the red wine pears: Peel pears, cut in half, core, and braise pears in red wine with sugar for about 20 minutes until al dente.

Season game gravy once again to taste before serving and distribute on plates with the meat. Arrange red wine pears next to the meat and garnish each pear with 1 tsp cranberry sauce.

☞ Goes with a green salad and dumplings or buttered noodles.

Pork Chops with Onions and Apples

4 pork chops, Salt, Freshly ground black pepper, 4 tbs vegetable oil
For the sauce: 2 onions, 2 apples, 1 tbs butter,
50 sour cherries with juice (from a jar)

Pound pork chops lightly on both sides and season with salt and pepper. In a large pan, heat oil and fry chops for 5–8 minutes on each side. Transfer to a plate and cover with aluminum foil.

For the sauce: Peel onions, cut in half, and then into strips. Peel apples, cut into quarters, core, and cut into small slices.

Add butter to pan residues and sauté onions and apples for 10 minutes, stirring repeatedly. Season with salt and pepper. Add meat juices from the chops you set aside and stir in sour cherries and juice. Transfer pork chops to 4 plates and top with the onion-apple mixture.

☞ You can also add 7 oz heavy cream to the onion-apple mixture and serve as a thick and creamy sauce. Or place a slice of cheese (e.g., Gouda or Emmenthaler cheese) on top of the chops and heat under the broiler.

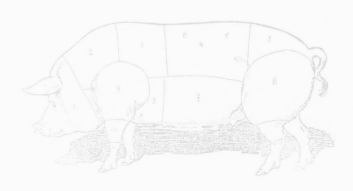

Veal Chops with Pear Gorgonzola Sauce

*1 pear (e.g., Bosc), ⅔ cup dry white wine, 1 tsp sugar, 1 whole clove,
1 onion, 1 tbs butter, 7 oz meat stock, 7 oz heavy cream,
1 bay leaf, Salt, Freshly ground black pepper, 4 veal chops,
5 tbs vegetable oil, ⅔ cup Gorgonzola cheese*

Peel pear, cut lengthwise into quarters, and core. In a saucepan, combine 7 oz water, 3½ tbs white wine, sugar and clove, and bring to a boil. Add pear quarters and simmer over low heat for 8–10 minutes.

In the meantime, peel and mince onion. In a saucepan, heat butter until foamy and braise minced onion until translucent. Add stock and half the cream. Add bay leaf, season lightly with salt and pepper, and simmer gently for about 10 minutes.

In the meantime, lightly pound veal chops and season with salt and pepper. In a large pan, heat oil and slowly sauté meat on both sides. Transfer cooked chops to a plate and cover with aluminum foil. Briefly bring pan residues and remaining wine to a boil and pour pan contents into the sauce. Remove bay leaf. Add remaining cream and Gorgonzola in small pieces. Purée with a hand blender and add more seasoning to taste.

Transfer veal chops to preheated plates. Cut each quarter pear lengthwise into thin slices and arrange in a fan pattern on top of the chops. Top with sauce and serve immediately.

☞ If desired, brown in a preheated oven set to the broiler setting.

Chicken Steaks with Apple Pear Sauce

*1 small onion, 1 apple, ½ pear, 4 chicken steaks (about 6¼ oz each),
2 tbs vegetable oil, Salt, Freshly ground white pepper, 1 tbs butter,
7 oz heavy cream, 3½ tbs apricot jam
For the marinade: 1 onion, 1 clove garlic, 5 tbs vegetable oil,
½ tsp dried marjoram, 7 tbs apricot jam, heated, 7 tbs tomato ketchup,
2 tbs soy sauce, 1 tsp mild curry powder, ¼ tsp black peppercorns*

For the marinade: Peel onion and garlic and cut into strips. Sauté in hot oil for several minutes, remove, and combine with marjoram, apricot jam, ketchup, soy sauce, curry, and peppercorns. Pour this marinade onto chicken steaks, cover, and refrigerate for at least 8 hours.

Then peel onion, apple, and pear. Mince onion. Core and chop apple and pear. Remove chicken steaks from marinade and lightly strip off excess. Sauté steaks in hot vegetable oil on both sides for 3–4 minutes. Transfer to a plate, season with salt and pepper, and cover with aluminum foil.

Add butter to pan residues and briefly braise onion, apple, and pear for 5 minutes, stirring repeatedly. Add cream and stir in apricot jam. Return to a boil and then simmer over medium heat for 5 minutes. Add more seasoning to taste and stir in meat juices from the chicken you set aside. Arrange steaks on preheated plates. Using a hand blender, purée sauce until creamy and pour over the chicken.

☞ Tastes best with wild rice and a green salad.

Scandinavian-Style Meatloaf

2 two-day-old bread rolls, 1 onion, 1 apple, 1 cucumber,
3 tbs sliced pickled beets, 3½ tbs raisins, 4 tsp aquavit (Scandinavian
liquor), 1 tbs butter, 1 lb ground meat (half pork, half beef), 1 egg,
Salt, Freshly ground black pepper, 5 tbs vegetable oil, 7 tbs meat stock
For the sauce: 1 cup sour cream, 1 tbs medium-hot mustard,
1 tsp tomato paste, 1 small apple,
Salt, Freshly ground black pepper

Soften rolls in water. Peel and mince onion. Peel apple, cut into quarters, core, and dice. Finely dice cucumber and beet slices. Pour aquavit over raisins. In a pan, heat butter and briefly braise onion and apple. Let cool.

Squeeze out rolls thoroughly and knead together with ground meat, egg, onion, apple, cucumber, beets, and raisins. Season mixture with salt and pepper and shape into a loaf.

In a roasting pan, heat oil and brown meatloaf on all sides. Roast in an oven pre-heated to 425°F for about 50 minutes, occasionally sprinkling with a little stock.

Remove meatloaf from the oven and let stand for 5–10 minutes. In the meantime, make the sauce: Combine sour cream, mustard, and tomato paste. Peel apple, grate finely, and add. Season with salt and pepper. Cut meatloaf into thick slices, arrange on plates, and serve sauce on the side.

☞ Delicious with mashed potatoes, deep-fried onion rings, and a mixed green salad.

Apples Stuffed with Ground Meat

3½ tbs slivered almonds, 4 apples of equal size, 1 tsp sugar,
Juice of 1 lemon, 6–8 fresh mint leaves, 7 tbs plain yogurt,
3½ tbs raisins, ⅔ cup hot meat stock, 1 onion,
2 tbs vegetable oil, 1 cup ground lamb, Salt,
Freshly ground black pepper, 1 dash cumin, 1 dash coriander
Plus: Butter for the casserole dish

In a hot, ungreased pan, lightly toast slivered almonds while stirring, then transfer to a plate. Rinse apples (do not peel) and remove a wide margin of core using an apple corer. Place in a bowl and sprinkle with sugar. Add lemon juice and enough cold water to cover the apples.

Rinse mint leaves, pat dry, cut into strips, and stir into yogurt. Pour 3½ tbs meat stock onto raisins. Peel and mince onion. In a pan, heat oil and briefly braise minced onion. Add ground meat and simmer while stirring until crumbly. Season with salt, pepper, cumin and coriander, and add remaining stock. Simmer over low heat for 5–8 minutes, then remove from heat, and stir in slivered almonds, raisins, and mint yogurt. Add more seasoning to taste.

Remove apples from water, place in a buttered casserole dish, and stuff with meat mixture. Bake in an oven preheated to 400°F for about 30 minutes until golden brown.

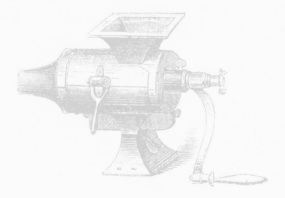

Berlin-Style Liver

2 onions, 2 apples, 3½ tbs butter, 1 pinch dried marjoram,
4 slices calf's liver, 2 tbs flour, 1 tbs vegetable oil, Salt,
7 tbs veal stock, 3½ tbs sour cream

Peel onions, cut in half, and then into strips. Peel apples, cut into quarters, core, and cut into wedges. In a pan, heat half the butter, sear onion strips, transfer to a platter, and keep warm. Add remaining butter to pan residues and sauté apple wedges on all sides. Season with marjoram and add to the onions. Dredge liver slices in flour. Add oil to pan residues and sauté liver slices on both sides for about 4 minutes. Place on top of onions and apples and salt lightly. Add veal stock to pan residues, briefly bring to a boil, and enrich with sour cream. Spoon over calf's liver.

Rice with Pork Cutlet Strips and Apple

14 oz pork cutlet, 1 onion, 1 apple, 4 tbs vegetable oil,
Salt, Freshly ground black pepper, 1 tbs butter,
3 tbs Calvados (apple brandy),
1¾ cup cooked rice (from previous day),
½ tsp marjoram, 4 tbs barbecue sauce

Cut cutlets into very thin strips. Peel onion. Peel and core apple. Cut onion and apple into strips. In a pan, heat oil and sear meat strips on all sides in several batches. Transfer to a plate and season with salt and pepper.

Add butter to the pan residues and braise onion and apple strips for several minutes. Add Calvados and stir in rice. Season pan contents with salt, pepper, and marjoram. Fold in meat strips and season to taste with barbecue sauce. Serve immediately.

Potato and Bacon Noodles on Apple Onion Sauce

For the noodles: 1 ²/₃ lb floury potatoes, Salt,
3¹/₂ oz smoked bacon, 2 egg yolks, Freshly ground black pepper,
1 pinch grated nutmeg, 2 tbs flour
For the apple onion sauce: 1 large onion, 1 apple,
1 tbs butter, 7 tbs gravy (or prepackaged gravy)
Plus: Flour for shaping dough, 3¹/₂ tbs clarified butter for sautéing

For the noodles: Rinse potatoes, peel, and cook in salted water until done. Finely dice smoked bacon and render in a hot pan. Remove pan from heat and let bacon cool. While potatoes are still hot, put through a ricer and let cool. Combine potatoes, egg yolks, bacon, salt, pepper and nutmeg, and knead into a pliable dough.

Dust your hands with flour and shape dough into finger-sized noodles. Place on a plate, cover with plastic wrap, and refrigerate for about 1 hour.

In the meantime, make the sauce: Peel onion and cut into fine strips. Peel apple, core, and cut into small slices. In a pan, heat butter and braise onion strips until translucent. Add apple slices and braise for another 5 minutes. Add gravy. Gently simmer over low heat for 8–10 minutes.

In a large pan, heat clarified butter and sauté noodles on all sides until golden brown and crispy. Distribute apple onion sauce on plates and top with noodles.

☞ Kids really love this one!

Marinated Fish and Vegetables

1½ lb fish fillets (e.g., cod, red snapper), Juice of ½ lemon, Salt,
Freshly ground black pepper, 2 small carrots, 1 onion, 1 leek,
1 green bell pepper, 1 small red chile pepper, 2 tart apples, 8 tbs olive oil,
2 tbs brown sugar, 1 tbs black peppercorns, 2 whole cloves, 2 bay leaves,
1 pinch each of cinnamon, cardamom, and nutmeg,
7 oz dry white wine, 2 tbs white wine vinegar

Rinse fish fillets, pat dry, drizzle with lemon juice, and season with salt and pepper. Peel carrots and onion and cut into fine strips. Cut leek in half lengthwise, rinse between the leaves, and cut crosswise into fine strips. Remove stems, seeds, and interiors from bell pepper and chile pepper, and cut into strips. Peel apples, cut into quarters, core, and slice.

In a large pan, heat half the olive oil and sauté fish fillets on both sides for 5 minutes. Remove and arrange side by side on a plate. Add remaining olive oil to the pan residues and briefly braise carrots, onion, leek, bell pepper, chile pepper, and apples. Sprinkle with sugar, let caramelize briefly, and stir in spices. Add white wine and white wine vinegar. Braise vegetables over low heat for 5 minutes. Place alternating layers of fish and vegetables in a shallow casserole dish, finishing with a layer of vegetables. Cover with plastic wrap and refrigerate for at least 2 hours.

Serve cold with an oven-fresh baguette or herb baguette.

Apple Rice Pot with Shrimp

*⅔ lb cooked, peeled shrimp (about 10½ oz), Juice of ½ lemon,
1 onion, 2 cloves garlic, 1 chile pepper, 2 apples,
1 banana, 4 tbs vegetable oil, ⅔ lb long-grain rice (about 10½ oz),
1 small jar saffron, Salt, Freshly ground pepper,
4 cups vegetable stock, 3½ tbs grated coconut*

Rinse shrimp, pat dry, and drizzle with lemon juice. Peel and mince onion and garlic. Remove stem, seeds and interiors from chile pepper, and dice finely. Peel apples, cut into quarters, core, and slice. Peel and slice banana.

In a large saucepan, heat vegetable oil and briefly braise onion, garlic, and chile pepper. Add apples and banana and braise for 5 minutes while stirring. Sprinkle in rice and season with saffron, salt, and pepper. Add stock and briefly bring to a boil. Cover the pan and cook rice over low heat for about 20 minutes, stirring occasionally. Fold shrimp and grated coconut into rice. Add more seasoning to taste and let rice pot stand uncovered for 5 minutes before serving.

☞ To make the rice pot more exotic, fold in 1 tbs chopped cilantro.

Potato Apple Purée

*1 2/3 lb potatoes, Salt, 2 apples (e.g., Golden Delicious),
3 1/2 tbs dry white wine, 1 tsp lemon juice,
1 tbs sugar, 2/3 cup softened butter,
Freshly ground white pepper, 1 pinch grated nutmeg*

Rinse potatoes, peel, and cook in salted water for about 25 minutes until done. In the meantime, peel apples, core, and cut into pieces about ⅛-inch thick. Place apple pieces in 3½ tbs water with white wine, lemon juice and sugar, and cook for 5–8 minutes until al dente.

Drain potatoes and put through a ricer. Stir in butter and apple pieces. Season purée with salt, pepper, and nutmeg.

☞ Garnish purée with browned onion rings and serve with liver or other meat dishes and with lots of gravy.

Grilled Apple Rings

*2 large apples (e.g., Rome Beauty or Granny Smith),
Juice of ½ lemon, 1 tbs melted butter, 1 tbs sugar*

Peel apples and remove a wide margin of core using an apple corer. Cut into rings about ⅜-inch thick and drizzle with lemon juice.

Line a baking sheet with aluminum foil and lay apple rings on the sheet side by side. Spread with butter and sprinkle with sugar. Preheat oven to 400°F, set to broil, and broil apples for 3–5 minutes.

☞ Use either as garnish for game dishes or as a dessert. In the latter case, serve Grilled Apple Rings with vanilla ice cream and rum raisins.

Deep-Fried Apple and Pear Pieces with Plum Sauce

1 lb apples, 1 lb pears, Juice of 1 lemon, 4 cups vegetable oil
For the plum sauce: 1 small onion, 2 cloves garlic,
3½ tbs smoked bacon, 1 small chile pepper, 1 tbs butter,
1 cup plum compote (from a jar), 4 tbs tomato ketchup, 4 tbs chile sauce,
1 tbs sugar, 1 tbs red wine vinegar, Salt, Freshly ground black pepper,
1 dash each of cinnamon, ginger, and mace
For the batter: 2 eggs, 7 oz flour, 7 oz dry white wine,
2 tbs melted butter, Salt, 1 pinch ground saffron

For the plum sauce, peel and mince onion and garlic. Finely dice bacon. Remove stem, seeds, and interior from chile pepper and chop finely. In a saucepan, heat butter until foamy and briefly braise onion, garlic, bacon, and chile pepper. Add plum compote and boil thoroughly for about 10 minutes while stirring frequently. Put sauce through a strainer and reheat. Season with tomato ketchup, chile sauce, sugar, vinegar, salt, pepper, cinnamon, ginger, and mace. Set aside.

For the batter, separate eggs and beat egg whites until stiff. Beat egg yolks, flour, white wine, and butter to form a thick batter. Season with salt and saffron, then fold in egg whites. Peel apples and pears and remove a wide margin of core using an apple corer. Cut fruit into rings about ¼-inch thick and drizzle with lemon juice. In a large saucepan or deep fryer, heat vegetable oil until scalding hot. Dip apple and pear rings into batter one at a time and place gently in the hot oil. Fry on both sides until golden. Remove with a slotted spoon, drain on paper towels, and arrange on a platter. Distribute sauce in individual bowls for each guest.

☞ Replace half the pears with onions to achieve a hearty, fruity flavor that is unforgettable when combined with the exotic plum sauce. Serve with white bread. This dish is also suitable as a side dish with grilled meats such as spare ribs, roast suckling pig, or grilled turkey.

Red Cabbage with Cinnamon Oranges and Apples

2¼ lb red cabbage, 7 oz orange juice, 2 tbs cranberry sauce,
A little grated lemon peel, 1 dash ground cinnamon, 2 apples,
1 tbs sugar, 7 tbs dry red wine, 3 whole cloves, 1 bay leaf,
1 large onion, 3½ tbs clarified butter, 1 cup meat stock, Salt,
Freshly ground black pepper, 1 tsp sugar, 1 tsp red wine vinegar

Clean red cabbage and cut into strips using a kitchen slicer. In a bowl, combine cabbage, orange juice, cranberry sauce, lemon peel, and cinnamon. Peel apples, core, and cut into strips. Add to cabbage along with sugar, red wine, cloves, and bay leaf. Cover bowl with plastic wrap and marinate in the refrigerator for 1 day.

Peel onion, cut in half, and then into strips. In a large saucepan, heat clarified butter and briefly braise onion strips. Stir in marinated red cabbage, pour in meat stock, and stew over low heat for about 1 hour. Just before it's done, season to taste with salt, pepper, sugar, and vinegar.

☞ Delicious with duck and goose dishes.

FRUITY CAKES AND PASTRIES

Pear and Pine Nut Muffins

Makes about 20 muffins
1 cup pears, 1 tbs pear brandy, 1⅓ cups flour, 1 tsp vanilla extract,
3 tsp baking powder, 1 pinch cloves, 7 tbs finely chopped pine nuts,
1 egg, ⅔ cup sugar, 7 tbs vegetable oil, 7 oz buttermilk
Plus: 20–24 paper baking cups, 1 tbs pine nuts for garnish,
Powdered sugar for decoration

Peel pears, cut into quarters, remove cores, cut into small cubes, and drizzle with brandy. In a bowl, combine flour, vanilla, baking powder, and cloves. Add pears and pine nuts.

In a second bowl, beat egg and sugar with an electric hand mixer until thick and creamy. Gradually beat in vegetable oil and buttermilk. Then fold in flour mixture. Line 2 muffin tins with paper baking cups, fill each cup ⅔ full with batter, sprinkle with pine nuts, and bake in an oven preheated to 350°F for 30–35 minutes. Remove from the oven and let stand for 5–10 minutes. Dust with powdered sugar and serve.

Apple Cranberry Muffins

Makes about 20 muffins (3-inch diameter)
1 cup apples, 3½ tbs cranberries, 7 oz whole-wheat flour,
7 tbs white flour, 3 tsp baking powder, 3½ tbs ground almonds, 1 egg,
⅔ cup brown sugar, 3½ tbs softened butter, 1¾ cups sour cream
Plus: 20–24 paper baking cups

Peel apples, cut into quarters, remove cores, dice finely, and combine with cran-berries. In a bowl, combine both types of flour, baking powder, and almonds.

In a second bowl, beat egg, sugar, butter, and sour cream with an electric hand mixer. Stir in apples, cranberries, and the flour mixture.

Line 2 muffin tins with paper baking cups, fill each cup ⅔ full with batter, and bake in an oven preheated to 350°F for about 25 minutes. Remove from the oven and let stand for 10 minutes before serving.

☞ If you want your muffins to rise more, add ½–1 tsp baking soda to the flour.
☞ You can vary this recipe with additional ingredients. My favorite version uses apples drizzled with amaretto and mixed with slivered almonds.

Apples in Nightgowns

4 medium apples, 2 tbs white rum, 1 tsp lemon juice, 3½ tbs sugar,
4 sheets frozen puff pastry dough (thawed), 3½ tbs ground almonds,
7 tbs currant jelly, 16 whole cloves, 1 egg yolk, 1 tbs melted butter
Plus: Flour for the work surface, 1 cup heavy cream,
1 large pinch cinnamon

Peel apples and remove a wide margin of core using an apple corer. Combine rum, lemon juice and sugar, and brush this mixture onto apples.

Lightly roll out pastry sheets on a floured work surface and place 1 apple in the center of each sheet. Fill holes in apples with 1 tsp ground almonds with a little current jelly on top.

Bring the corners of the pastry sheets together above the apple and seal edges tightly together. Fasten each corner to the apple with a clove. Mix egg yolk and butter, brush onto apples, and place apples on a baking sheet. Bake in an oven preheated to 400°F for about 20 minutes until golden. Just before serving, whip cream with cinnamon until stiff and serve with the apples.

☞ Apples in Nightgowns are a fantastic, fruity idea for afternoon coffee or dessert. If you don't especially like the flavor of rum, simply substitute apple juice, lemon juice, or white wine.

Crispy Apple Pockets

For the dough: 1 lb flour, 7 oz lukewarm milk,
3½ tbs sugar, 1 pkg dry yeast, 7 tbs softened butter,
1 tsp grated lemon peel, 1 pinch salt, 1 pinch cinnamon
For the filling: 3½ tbs raisins, 1 tbs rum, 1 lb apples,
Juice of ½ lemon, 3½ tbs sugar, 1 tsp vanilla extract
Plus: Flour for the work surface, Grease for the baking sheet,
1 egg yolk, 1 tbs melted butter, Powdered sugar for decoration

For the dough: Sift flour into a bowl. Make a well in the center, pour in milk, and sprinkle in sugar. Add dry yeast into the well, stir briefly, and dust with flour from the edges. Let pre-dough rise for about 20 minutes, then add butter, lemon peel, salt and cinnamon, and knead into a smooth dough. Cover and let rise for another 30 minutes.

In the meantime, make the filling: Pour rum over raisins. Peel apples, cut into quarters, core, and cut into cubes of about ¼ inch. In a saucepan, combine apples, lemon juice, sugar, vanilla and rum raisins, and braise for 5 minutes while stirring. Transfer apple mixture to a plate and let cool.

Knead dough thoroughly on a floured work surface and roll it out. Cut dough into squares of about 4 x 4 inch and place a little filling in the center of each. Fold corners together over the filling and press edges firmly together. Place all the apple pockets on a greased baking sheet and bake in an oven preheated to 400°F for about 20 minutes. Remove, let cool, and decorate with a thick coating of powdered sugar.

☞ If children are eating with you, pour a mixed fruit juice onto the raisins instead of rum.

Bavarian Apple Strudel

For the strudel dough: 1 cup flour, Salt,
4½ oz lukewarm water, 3 tbs vegetable oil
For the filling: 3½ cups tart apples (about 1¾ lb; e.g., Granny Smith),
Juice of 1 lemon, 7 tbs raisins, 7 tbs sugar, 2 tbs rum (optional),
7 tbs sour cream, 1 tbs breadcrumbs,
2 tbs melted butter, 7 oz heavy cream
Plus: Flour for sprinkling and for the work surface,
Butter for the baking sheet, Powdered sugar for decoration

For the strudel dough: Sift flour and salt onto a work surface. With the back of your hand, make a well in the center and quickly work in water and oil. Knead into a smooth dough, wrap in plastic wrap, and set aside for about 30 minutes.

In the meantime, make the filling: Peel apples, cut into quarters, core, and slice. In a bowl, combine apples, lemon juice, raisins, sugar, and rum, if desired.

Dust a kitchen towel with flour and roll out strudel dough into a thin sheet almost the same size as the towel. Spread surface with sour cream and sprinkle with breadcrumbs. Distribute apple mixture on top, leaving a margin of about 3 inches around the edges. Fold in the edges, roll up the strudel with the aid of the towel, and lay it on a buttered baking sheet. Brush with melted butter and bake in an oven preheated to 400°F for about 50 minutes. While baking, drizzle strudel several times with cream. When done, let stand for 10 minutes, decorate with a thick coating of powdered sugar, and cut into broad pieces.

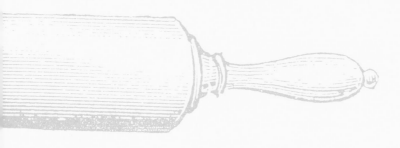

Almond Cake with Apples

2 medium apples, 1 tbs amaretto, ²⁄₃ cup softened butter, 7 tbs sugar,
1 tsp vanilla extract, A little grated lemon peel, 3 eggs, 5 tbs milk,
3 tsp baking powder, 7 oz flour, 3½ tbs ground almonds
Plus: Butter for the pan, 7 tbs apricot jam for spreading,
Powdered sugar for decoration

Peel apples, cut into quarters, core, cut into wedges, and drizzle with amaretto. In a bowl, combine butter, sugar, vanilla and lemon peel, and beat until thick and creamy. Beat in eggs and milk. Last of all, combine baking powder and flour and fold into the mixture along with almonds.

Butter a loaf pan and pour in half the batter. Arrange apple wedges on top and cover with remaining batter. Bake in an oven preheated to 400°F for about 40 minutes. Remove from the oven, let cool in the pan for 10 minutes, and then carefully reverse out of the pan.

Heat apricot jam, put through a strainer, and use to glaze the cake. Let stand for about 10 minutes. Dust with a thick coating of powdered sugar and serve.

☞ You can also top the cake with a different glaze, such as a chocolate couverture.

Aunt Anni's Apple Cake

Makes 1 springform pan (11-inch diameter)
For the dough: 1 cup flour, 1 egg, ⅔ cup cold butter, cut into bits,
1 tbs sugar, Salt
For the filling: 3½ tbs raisins, 2 tbs rum, 2¼ lb apples,
Juice and a little grated peel of 1 lemon, 1 tbs sugar,
½ tsp cinnamon, 3½ tbs slivered almonds
For the frosting: 3 eggs, 3 tbs sugar, 2 tbs flour, 7 oz heavy cream
Plus: Flour for the work surface, Butter for the pan,
Powdered sugar for decoration

For the dough: Knead together flour, egg, butter bits, sugar, and a pinch of salt. Shape dough into a ball, wrap in plastic wrap, and refrigerate for 1 hour.

In the meantime, make the filling: Pour rum over raisins. Peel apples, cut into quarters, core, and cut in small, thin slices. In a bowl, combine lemon juice, lemon peel, sugar, and cinnamon.

Thoroughly knead dough once more on a floured work surface and roll out lightly. Line a springform pan, including the sides, with the dough. Pierce bottom several times with a fork. Distribute apple mixture and raisins evenly over the dough and sprinkle with slivered almonds. For the frosting: Combine eggs, sugar, flour and cream, and stir until smooth, and slowly pour onto filling. Bake in an oven preheated to 400°F for about 45 minutes. Remove from the oven and let cool in the pan for about 10 minutes. Dust with a thick coating of powdered sugar and serve.

☞ The entire preparation time (which always used to fly by in Aunt Anni's kitchen because of the constant gabbing that went on) is about 2½ hours. What better way to spend your time than baking and gossiping?

Fine Apple Cake

Makes 1 springform pan (10-inch diameter)
½ cup butter, ½ cup sugar, 3 eggs, Salt, Juice of ½ lemon,
7 oz flour, 1½ tsp baking powder, 4 tbs milk,
1 lb tart apples (e.g., Granny Smith)
Plus: Butter for the pan

Beat butter and sugar until fluffy. Gradually add eggs, salt, and lemon juice. Combine flour and baking powder and work into the butter mixture with a hand mixer. Add just enough milk so that when you let a spoonful fall back into the bowl, the batter separates very slowly from the spoon. Butter a springform pan, pour in batter, and smooth out the surface.

Peel apples, cut into quarters, core, and cut slits lengthwise into the apple quarters ⅛–³⁄₁₆ inch apart. Press quarters into the batter in concentric circles. Bake in an oven preheated to 400°F for 40–50 minutes.

Puff Pastry Cake with Marzipan Apples

1 lb apples, Juice of ½ lemon, 7 tbs apricot jam,
2 round sheets of frozen puff pastry dough (about a 12½-inch diameter),
7 oz marzipan, 7 tbs powdered sugar, 7 tbs mascarpone cheese,
2 eggs, 1 tbs sugar, 1 dash cinnamon

Peel apples, quarter, core, cut into thin wedges, and drizzle with lemon juice. In a saucepan, heat apricot jam while stirring constantly. Line 2 baking sheets with parchment paper. Place pastry dough sheets on top and spread with half the apricot jam. Set aside remaining jam.

Knead together marzipan and powdered sugar. Divide in half and roll out each half into a round sheet. Place marzipan sheets in the center of the pastry sheets. Arrange apple wedges on top in an overlapping pattern, starting from the center and working your way outward. Spread apple wedges with remaining apricot jam. Combine mascarpone, eggs, sugar and cinnamon, and stir until smooth and spoon over the 2 cakes. One at a time, place sheets on the middle rack of an oven preheated to 425°F and bake for 15–20 minutes until golden.

French Apple Cake

Makes 1 springform or tart pan (8½- to 10-inch diameter)
For the dough: ⅔ cup flour, 7 tbs cold butter, cut into bits,
1 large pinch salt, 1 tbs sugar, 1 egg yolk
For the topping: 4 apples, 2 tbs apple jelly (recipe on page 106)
Plus: Butter for the pan, Flour for the work surface

For the dough: Quickly knead flour, butter bits, salt, sugar, egg yolk, and about 3½ tbs cold water into a smooth dough.

Butter a springform pan. Lightly roll out dough on a floured work surface. Press dough into the bottom of the pan and ¾ inch up the sides.

Peel apples, cut into quarters, remove seeds, and cut into thin wedges. Arrange on the dough in an overlapping pattern. Slightly heat apple jelly and spread over apples. Bake cake in an oven preheated to 400°F for about 40 minutes until golden. Serve warm or cold.

☞ Instead of apple jelly, you can also use apricot jam.

Yeast Dough Fruit Cake

Makes 1 springform pan (8½-inch diameter)
For the dough: 7 tbs sugar, 7 tbs softened butter, 2 eggs,
7 tbs flour, 1 pkg dry yeast, 1 pinch salt
For the topping: 2 small pears, 2 apples, 3 tbs sugar
Plus: Parchment paper and butter for the pan, Flour for the work surface,
1 tbs powdered sugar for decoration

For the dough: Beat sugar and butter until fluffy. Gradually add eggs, flour, dry yeast, salt, and about 4 tbs water. Let dough rise for about 15 minutes.

In the meantime, line a springform pan with parchment paper and grease the paper with butter. Peel pears and apples, cut into quarters, core, and cut into thin wedges.

Thoroughly knead dough once again and roll out to the size of the pan. Arrange pear and apple slices on the dough lining the pan and sprinkle evenly with sugar.

Bake in an oven preheated to 350°F for up to 1 hour until done. Remove from oven, let cool slightly, and dust with powdered sugar. Serve warm or cold.

Yogurt Apple Cream Torte

Makes 1 springform pan (8½-inch diameter)
For the dough: 7 oz flour, 3½ tbs lukewarm milk, 1 tsp sugar,
1 pkg dry yeast, Grated peel of 1½ lemons, 3 tbs melted butter
For the topping: 5 apples, 3½ tbs Calvados (apple brandy),
Juice of ¼ lemon, 1½ pkg powdered gelatin,
2¼ cups plain yogurt, 2 tbs sugar
Plus: Butter for the pan, Flour for the work surface

For the dough: Sift flour into a bowl and make a well in the center. Pour milk into well and mix with sugar and yeast. Set aside pre-dough for about 20 minutes. Then add lemon peel and butter and knead thoroughly. Cover bowl with a cloth and let rise in a warm place for another 30 minutes. In the meantime, make the topping: Peel apples, cut into quarters, core, and cut into wedges. Combine apple wedges, Calvados, and lemon juice.

Butter a springform pan. Thoroughly knead dough once again on a floured work surface, roll out, and completely line the pan with it. Drain apples well, setting aside the liquid, and arrange on the dough. Bake in an oven preheated to 400°F for 30–35 minutes. Remove and let cool in the pan.

Soften gelatin in cold water. Transfer wet gelatin to a heat-resistant bowl and dissolve over a hot double boiler while stirring. Combine yogurt, sugar, and Calvados-lemon mixture that was set aside. Fold in gelatin. Pour this cream over the apple cake and smooth out the surface. Refrigerate so it can become firm. Serve well chilled.

Sponge Roll with Pear Cream

For the pear cream: 2 pears, Juice of ½ lemon,
3½ tbs sugar, 3½ tbs white wine, 1 cup heavy cream,
1 tsp vanilla extract, 3½ tbs cranberry sauce
For the sponge batter: 2 eggs, 7 tbs sugar,
3 tbs lukewarm water, 6 tbs flour, 2 tbs cornstarch
Plus: Powdered sugar for decoration

For the pear cream: Peel pears, cut into quarters, and core. In a saucepan, combine lemon juice, sugar and white wine, and add pears. Pour in just enough water to cover the fruit. Bring to a boil and simmer over medium heat for 5 minutes. Remove from heat and let cool.

For the sponge batter: Separate eggs. Beat egg whites until stiff. Beat egg yolks with sugar and lukewarm water until foamy. Fold in egg whites. Sift flour and cornstarch onto the egg mixture and stir. Line a baking sheet with parchment paper, pour on sponge batter, and smooth out the surface. Bake in an oven preheated to 350°F for 7–8 minutes.

In the meantime, whip cream with vanilla until stiff and lightly fold in cranberry sauce. Cut pear quarters into small pieces or slices. Pat dry with paper towels, if necessary, and fold into cream.

Remove baking sheet from the oven and reverse sponge onto a damp kitchen towel. Moisten parchment paper slightly and remove. Spread pear cream onto sponge cake, leaving a margin around the edges. With the aid of the kitchen towel, roll up sponge from one of the long edges so that the seam is under the roll. Leave the roll wrapped in the kitchen towel for about 15 minutes so it will retain its shape. Remove kitchen towel. Place sponge roll on a cutting or serving board and dust liberally with powdered sugar.

Chocolate Sour Cream Cake with Pears

Makes 1 springform pan (8½-inch diameter)
3 large pears, 3 tbs pear brandy, 4 eggs, 3 tbs sugar,
1 box chocolate pudding mix (about 3 oz),
3½ tbs pear juice, 4¼ cups low-fat sour cream (about 35 oz)
Plus: Butter and breadcrumbs for the pan, Powdered sugar for decoration

Peel pears, cut into quarters, core, and cut into cubes of about ⅜ inch. Pour brandy over pears and marinate. Separate eggs and beat egg whites with sugar until stiff. Stir pudding mix and pear juice until smooth. Beat egg yolks until thick and creamy, then stir in chocolate cream, and sour cream. Add drained pear pieces and, finally, fold in egg whites.

Butter a springform pan, sprinkle with breadcrumbs, and pour in batter. Bake in an oven preheated to 325°F for about 30 minutes. Then raise the temperature to 400°F and bake for another 40 minutes. Switch off oven and let cake cool in the oven. Dust with powdered sugar.

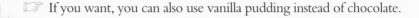 If you want, you can also use vanilla pudding instead of chocolate.

DESSERTS AND TREATS

Apple Sauce

1 lb tart apples (e.g., Granny Smith), 7 tbs sugar

Peel apples, cut into quarters, core, and cut into small pieces. Heat with 3 tbs water and boil until tender. Put through a strainer, stir in sugar, and let cool.

☞ You can also add cinnamon and a little lemon juice, if desired.

Apple Sauce with Cinnamon Mascarpone

1 lb apples, 3½ tbs sugar, Juice of 1 lemon, ½ stick cinnamon,
4 whole cloves, 3½ tbs mascarpone cheese,
3½ tbs heavy cream, 1 dash cinnamon

Peel apples, cut into quarters, core, and cut into wedges. In a saucepan, combine sugar, lemon juice and 1 cup water, and bring to a boil. Add apple wedges, cinnamon stick, and cloves. Simmer over low heat for 10-15 minutes until tender. Remove cinnamon stick and cloves. If desired, purée apples either finely or coarsely with a hand blender. Transfer to individual bowls when either warm or well cooled. Combine mascarpone, cream and cinnamon, and stir until smooth. Place 1 tbs of mascarpone-cinnamon mixture on top of each serving of apple sauce.

☞ If you're counting calories, you can replace the sugar with a liquid sweetener.

Apple Compote

7 oz tart apples (e.g., Granny Smith), 3½ tbs sugar

Lemon juice or white wine, as desired

Peel apples, cut into ¼ or ⅛, and core. Combine 1 cup water and sugar, bring to a boil, add apples, and simmer until done but not too tender. Let cool and season to taste with sugar and lemon juice or white wine.

Emperor's Apple Pancakes

3 eggs, ⅔ cup flour, 7 oz milk, 4¼ tbs melted butter, 2 apples,
3½ tbs slivered almonds, 1–2 tbs powdered sugar
Plus: Powdered sugar for decoration

For the batter: Separate eggs. Using an electric hand mixer, beat flour, milk, egg yolks, and 4¼ tsp melted butter until smooth. Beat egg whites until stiff and fold in. Peel apples, cut into quarters, core, and cut into bite-sized pieces.

Heat wok on the stove. Add 4¼ tsp butter and stir-fry half the apple pieces and half the slivered almonds. Dust with about 1 tsp powdered sugar, caramelize briefly, and pour half the batter onto the contents of the wok. When batter has set, scramble and turn with 2 wooden spoons. Fry batter pieces until golden brown on all sides and transfer to a platter. Add remaining butter to pan residues and repeat procedure with remaining ingredients. Dust pancakes with a thick coating of powdered sugar and serve immediately.

☞ Goes with plum compote or warm plum wine, canned pear pieces, or apple sauce (recipe on page 81).
☞ You don't necessarily have to use a wok; a large nonstick pan will work almost as well.
☞ If you want, you can replace slivered almonds with sliced hazelnuts or chopped macadamia nuts. You can also add rum-soaked raisins or plain raisins.

Apple Pancakes

⅔ cup flour, 6 eggs, 2 cups milk, 2 tbs sugar, 1 pinch salt,
1 lb tart apples (e.g., Granny Smith), 4 tbs butter
Plus: 1 dash cinnamon, 4 tbs sugar

Beat flour, eggs, milk, sugar, and salt into a smooth batter. If it contains any lumps, put the batter through a strainer. Let stand for 20 minutes. Peel apples, cut into quarters, core, and cut into wedges.

In a pan, heat a little butter and pour in ¼ of the batter. Distribute ¼ of the apple wedges on top. Fry pancake until the underside is golden brown. Carefully slide onto a plate. Add a little more butter to the pan and return pancake to fry the other side. When done, remove from pan and keep warm. Repeat the procedure to prepare remaining 3 pancakes. Combine cinnamon and sugar and sprinkle over pancakes before serving.

Dried Apple Rings

2¼ lb apples (e.g., Cortland, Rome Beauty), Juice of 1 lemon

Peel apples and remove a wide margin of core using an apple corer. Cut cross-wise into rings ¼-inch thick. Bring water with lemon juice to a boil. Add apple rings and return to a boil. Then remove, drain, and spread them out on an oven rack. Place the rack in an oven preheated to 120°F and dry apples. The rings are done when you can break them and no juice emerges.

☞ Make sure the dried apple rings are completely dry before you transfer them to air-tight jars for storage.
☞ Chocolate lovers can also coat dried apple rings with melted chocolate.
☞ Instead of apples, use pears.

Apples à la Pirandello

This wonderful recipe is considered a classic, although it has slowly been disappearing from international menus over the last few years. It was dedicated to the Italian playwright Luigi Pirandello (1867-1936), who may have been inspired by this "sweet sin" to write a novella, comedy, or novel.

4 apples, 3½ tbs sugar, Juice of ½ lemon
For the filling: 7 tbs finely diced candied orange peel and candied lemon
peel, 3 tbs cherry brandy, 3 tbs maraschino liqueur, 7 tbs apricot jam
For serving: 4 scoops vanilla ice cream, 7 tbs raspberry jam,
1 cup heavy cream

Peel apples and remove a wide margin of core using an apple corer. Combine sugar, lemon juice, and 2 cups water, bring to a boil and add apples. Pour in just enough water to cover apples. Return to a boil, cook gently for about 5 minutes, and then let cool in the water.

For the filling: Combine candied orange peel, candied lemon peel, cherry brandy, and maraschino liqueur. Slightly heat apricot jam and stir into this mixture. Drain apples and fill with mixture. Place a scoop of ice cream in each center of 4 dessert plates and place 1 stuffed apple on top, flattening the ice cream a little. Heat raspberry jam while stirring and put through a strainer. Spread jam all over the apples. Whip cream until stiff, place in a pastry bag, and use to decorate the apples. Pipe whipped cream rosettes all around the apples.

☞ You can also drizzle chocolate or raspberry sauce onto the apples.

Deep-Fried Caramel Apples on a Stick

2 eggs, 3½ tbs flour, 3½ tbs cornstarch, 8 small apples,
1½ qt vegetable oil, 7 tbs sugar
Plus: 16 wooden skewers

For the batter: With an electric hand mixer set to the highest speed, beat eggs, flour, cornstarch, and 5 tbs cold water until smooth.

Peel apples and core with an apple corer. In a large saucepan, heat oil. One at a time, dip apples into the batter, float in the oil, and deep-fry for about 3 minutes until golden brown. Remove with a slotted spoon and drain on a cooling rack.

Place 2 tbs of the frying oil in a pan, sprinkle in sugar, and caramelize while stirring. Pierce each fried apple with 2 wooden skewers and spoon on the caramel coating. Let harden briefly, then bite, and enjoy.

☞ You can also pierce washed and dried apples with wooden sticks and dip into the caramel. Children love these caramel apples.

Red Love Apples

4 apples, 2 cups sugar, 1 tsp red food coloring, 1 tsp white vinegar
Plus: 4 long, thick, wooden sticks

Remove stems from apples, rinse, dry with paper towels, and pierce each with a wooden stick. Sprinkle 7 tbs sugar on a plate. In a saucepan, dissolve remaining sugar with food coloring, vinegar, and 5 tbs water while stirring constantly with a wooden spoon and reduce to a thick syrup. One at a time, dip apples in the syrup, turning them with the wooden stick until they are completely covered. Then place red caramel apples on the plate of sugar to harden with the stick pointing up.

☞ Always a favorite, and not just with children.

Tipsy Fried Apple Rings in an Almond Crust

3 apples (Granny Smith or Gravenstein), Juice of ½ lemon, 2 tbs rum
For the batter: 2 eggs, 7 oz flour, Salt, 3½ tbs sugar,
1 tbs vegetable oil, 7 oz pale beer, 3½ tbs slivered almonds
Plus: 1 lb clarified butter, 7 tbs sugar, 1 tsp cinnamon

Peel apples, remove a wide margin of core using an apple corer, and cut into rings about ⅜-inch thick. Place in a bowl and drizzle with lemon juice and rum.

For the batter: Separate eggs. Beat egg whites until stiff and refrigerate until you need them. In a bowl, combine flour, salt, sugar, egg yolks, vegetable oil and beer, and stir to form a thick batter. Fold in egg whites.

In a large saucepan or deep frying pan, heat clarified butter. One by one, dip apple rings into the batter, sprinkle with slivered almonds, float in the hot butter, and fry on both sides for 2–3 minutes until golden. Remove and drain on paper towels. Dredge apples in a mixture of sugar and cinnamon.

☞ Especially delicious with vanilla ice cream or vanilla sauce.

Almond Cream on a Bed of Apples

2 apples, 1 tsp lemon juice, 2 tbs sugar,
2 whole cloves, 7 tbs dry white wine
For the almond cream: 4 egg yolks, 2 tbs powdered sugar, ¼ cup amaretto
For garnish: 3½ tbs sliced almonds, 8 ladyfingers

Peel apples, cut into quarters, and core. In a saucepan, combine lemon juice, sugar, cloves, and white wine. Add apple quarters and just enough water to cover the apples. Bring to a boil and simmer over low heat for 5 minutes. Remove apples, drain, and cut into small, thin slices. Arrange slices on 4 large plates in an overlapping pattern, starting from the center and working your way outward. In a hot, ungreased pan, toast sliced almonds while stirring until they give off an aroma. Sprinkle half onto the bed of apples.

For the almond cream: Over a hot double boiler, beat egg yolks and powdered sugar until thick and creamy. Slowly pour in amaretto and continue stirring until it forms a frothy cream. Spoon over bed of apples and sprinkle with remaining sliced almonds. Place 2 ladyfingers on the side of each plate to serve as "spoons."

Cinnamon Cream with Apples

2 apples, 2 whole cloves, 1 tsp lemon juice, 7 tbs sugar,
¾ pkg powdered gelatin, 1 cup milk, ½ vanilla bean,
3 fresh egg yolks, ½ tsp cinnamon, 1 cup heavy cream

Peel apples, core, and cut into pieces of about ¼ inch. In a saucepan, combine apples, cloves, lemon juice, half the sugar and 7 oz water, and bring to a boil. Pour through a strainer and drain apple pieces well, removing cloves.

Soften gelatin in cold water. In a saucepan, combine milk and the pulp from the vanilla bean and bring to a boil, then remove from heat. In a heat-resistant bowl, beat egg yolks with remaining sugar until thick and creamy. Place the bowl over a hot double boiler. Slowly beat vanilla milk into the egg yolk-sugar mixture until the cream takes on a firm consistency. Squeeze out gelatin and dissolve in this mixture. Remove bowl from double boiler, beat briefly over ice water, and stir in cinnamon. Whip cream until stiff and carefully fold apples and whipped cream into the creamy mixture. Transfer cream to individual bowls, cover, and refrigerate for at least 1 hour.

☞ Serve with a shot of Calvados and an espresso.

Marzipan Mousse on Prosecco Apples

1 pkg powdered gelatin, 1 cup milk, 7 oz marzipan,
1 cup heavy cream, 1 egg yolk, 4 tsp amaretto, 2 apples,
7 oz Prosecco (or any brand of sparkling wine)

Soften gelatin in cold water. In a saucepan, heat milk and stir in marzipan until thick and creamy. Remove from heat and let cool.

In the meantime, whip cream until stiff. Stir egg yolk and amaretto into marzipan. Transfer wet gelatin to a heat-resistant bowl, place over a hot double boiler, dissolve while stirring, and add to marzipan. Finally, fold in whipped cream, cover with plastic wrap, and refrigerate for at least 2 hours.

Peel apples, cut into quarters, core, cut into wedges, and place in a saucepan. Pour in Prosecco and cook gently over low heat for about 10 minutes. Let apples cool in the Prosecco, then distribute in 4 shallow bowls. Use 2 tbs to transfer small mounds of marzipan mousse onto the apple wedges.

☞ Fill a pastry bag with chocolate sauce and drizzle thin lines back and forth across the top.
☞ Drink remaining Prosecco while preparing this treat or while eating it.

Apple Crêpes Babette

Crêpes Suzette with an orange filling are a classic. My friend Babette loves crêpes with apples— and I love her crêpes!

Makes 8 crêpes
2 apples, 1 tbs butter, 1 tbs sugar, 3½ tbs white wine, 1 tbs amaretto
For the crêpe batter: 7 oz milk, 7 tbs flour,
1 tsp vanilla extract, 2 eggs, 1 tbs melted butter
Plus: Butter for frying, 3 tbs brandy

Peel apples, core, cut into quarters, and then into narrow wedges. In a pan, heat butter until foamy and briefly swirl apple wedges around in the butter. Sprinkle with sugar, let caramelize, and add white wine and amaretto. Bring to a boil only briefly and then remove pan from heat.

For the crêpe batter: Using an electric hand mixer, beat milk, flour, vanilla, eggs, and butter until smooth and let stand for 20 minutes.

In a large pan with low sides or, even better, in a crêpe pan, heat a little butter. Ladle a small amount of batter into the pan and tip the pan so the batter runs evenly all over the bottom. Brown briefly, then turn carefully and brown lightly on the other side. Transfer to a plate and keep warm. Repeat this procedure with remaining batter.

Place 1 warm crêpe on each preheated plate. Top half with apples and fold over the other half. Pour brandy into a ladle and hold the bottom of the ladle over a flame to heat. Pour brandy evenly over the crêpes. Flambé each serving, preferably right at the table.

Apple Semolina Casserole with Raspberries

1 qt milk, Salt, ⅔ cup durum semolina,
3 large apples, ½ stick cinnamon, 2 whole cloves,
Grated peel and juice of ½ lemon, 3 eggs, 3½ tbs sugar,
⅔ cup frozen raspberries (thawed), 1 tsp powdered sugar
Plus: Butter for the casserole dish

Bring milk and salt to a boil. Stir in semolina, bring to a boil, and cook over low heat for 20 minutes, stirring frequently. Remove from heat and let cool briefly.

Peel apples, cut into quarters, core, and slice. In a saucepan, combine 7 tbs water, cinnamon stick, cloves, lemon peel and lemon juice, and bring to a boil. Remove from heat, add apples, and let stand for 5 minutes. Pour apples into a strainer and remove cinnamon stick and cloves. Separate eggs. Stir egg yolks and sugar into the semolina.

Butter a casserole dish and spread half the semolina onto the bottom. Place half the apples and the drained raspberries on top. Cover with remaining semolina and finish with the remaining apples. Beat egg whites with powdered sugar until stiff and spread onto casserole. Bake in an oven preheated to 400°F for about 20 minutes.

Apple Spice Ice Cream with Calvados Sauce

For the ice cream: ½ cup milk, 1½ cups heavy cream,
1 stick cinnamon, 2 whole cloves, 1 dash allspice, 2 eggs,
1 egg yolk, 2 tbs sugar, 1 apple, Juice of ¼ lemon
For the Calvados sauce: 2 egg yolks, 1 tbs sugar, 3 tbs white wine,
4 tsp Calvados (apple brandy)

For the ice cream: In a saucepan, combine milk, ½ cup cream, cinnamon stick, cloves and allspice, and bring to a boil. Remove from heat and let liquid cool. Remove cinnamon stick and cloves.

In a heat-resistant bowl, beat eggs, egg yolk, and sugar until thick and creamy. Place the bowl over a hot double boiler and slowly pour in milk–cream mixture while beating vigorously. Continue beating until it forms a thick and creamy mixture. Remove bowl from double boiler and beat briefly over ice water. Whip remaining cream until stiff and fold into egg mixture. Peel apples, cut in half, core, and grate finely with a kitchen grater. Mix with lemon juice and fold into egg mixture. Place apple spice cream in the freezer and freeze for at least 2 hours, stirring thoroughly 4 or 5 times over the course of the 2 hours.

Just before serving, make the Calvados sauce: In a heat-resistant bowl, beat egg yolks and sugar until thick and creamy. Place bowl over a hot double boiler and beat egg yolk cream with white wine and Calvados.

Take ice cream out of the freezer, thaw briefly, and transfer to dessert plates or ice cream bowls with a spoon or ice cream scoop. Pour warm Calvados sauce over the top.

☞ You can also sprinkle the ice cream with sliced almonds and rum raisins.
☞ If you have an ice cream maker, of course the ice cream will be perfect. But it tastes almost as good without a machine. Just don't forget to keep stirring it throughout the freezing process.

Pear Apple Pockets

*2¼ lb floury potatoes, Salt, 1 lb apples, 1 lb pears, Juice of 1 lemon,
7tbs sugar, 1 dash cinnamon, 1 egg, ⅔ cup cornstarch, 7 oz sour cream,
7 tbs half-and-half, 3½ tbs melted butter
Plus: Butter for the casserole dish, Flour for the work surface*

Rinse potatoes and cook in boiling, salted water for about 30 minutes. In the meantime, peel apples and pears, cut into quarters, core, cut into pieces of about ⅜ inch, and drizzle with lemon juice. Season with half the sugar and with cinnamon. Liberally butter a large casserole dish or broiler pan.

Drain potatoes, let cool enough to handle, peel, and put through a ricer. Process potatoes, egg, and cornstarch into a dough. Place potato dough on a floured work surface and shape into a roll about 10-inches long. Cut into slices about ¼-inch thick. Flatten each slice on the palm of your hand and place 1 tbs pear and apple pieces in the center. Fold the dough over into a semicircular pocket and seal the edges firmly. Hold pockets by the edge, set them down on the work surface with the seam side up, and press down lightly so they acquire a flattened base. Then set them in the casserole dish with the seam side up. Combine remaining sugar, sour cream, half-and-half and butter, and spoon over the pockets. Bake in an oven preheated to 400°F for 45–50 minutes until golden.

☞ Goes with a cranberry cream.
☞ If you don't have a lot of time, just buy frozen mashed potatoes from the supermarket.
☞ You can also make the filling out of apples alone or a mixture of apples and plums.

Poire Hélène

This culinary classic was named after the main character in the operetta "La belle Hélène," composed by Jacques Offenbach in 1864.

2 pears, 1 tbs sugar, 7 tbs dry white wine
For the chocolate sauce: 3½ tbs milk chocolate,
About 3½ tbs heavy cream
For serving: 8 small scoops ice cream, 2 tbs sliced almonds

Peel pears, cut in half, core, and place in a saucepan. Sprinkle sugar over the top, pour in white wine and 7 tbs water, and bring to a boil. As soon as it bubbles up, reduce the heat and simmer pear halves for 5 minutes.

In the meantime, break up chocolate. In a heat-resistant bowl, combine chocolate and cream and melt over a hot double boiler. Stir well and add more or less cream depending on how thick you want the sauce.

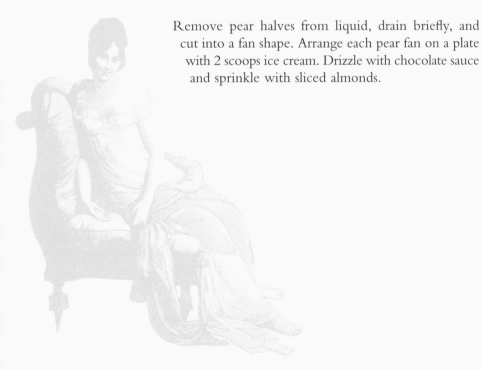

Remove pear halves from liquid, drain briefly, and cut into a fan shape. Arrange each pear fan on a plate with 2 scoops ice cream. Drizzle with chocolate sauce and sprinkle with sliced almonds.

Pears à la Casanova

Giacomo Girolamo Casanova (1725–1798) is known more for his love affairs than for his achievements. Who knows which lady seduced him with this dessert?

2 pears, 1 tsp lemon juice, 2 tbs sugar, 1 tsp vanilla extract,
1 cup heavy cream, 2 cups raspberry ice cream, 4 tbs Benedictine (French
cognac-based herb liqueur), 2 tbs chocolate sprinkles

Peel pears, cut in half, and core. In a saucepan, combine 2 cups water, lemon juice, sugar, and vanilla and bring to a boil. Add pears and as soon as the pan starts to boil, reduce heat, and cook gently for 5 minutes.

In the meantime, whip cream until stiff. Distribute raspberry ice cream in 4 individual bowls, smoothing it out to form a flat surface. Remove pear halves from the liquid, drain well, cut into a fan shape, and arrange on top. Drizzle 1 tbs Benedictine onto each pear, top with whipped cream, and decorate with chocolate sprinkles.

Red Wine Pears with Cinnamon Parfaits

For the cinnamon parfaits: 2 egg yolks, ½ tsp cinnamon,
3 tbs sugar, 1 cup heavy cream
For the red wine pears: 1 cup dry red wine, ⅔ cup sugar,
½ cinnamon stick, 2 whole cloves,
1 small pinch nutmeg, 4 small firm pears

For the cinnamon parfaits: Beat egg yolks, cinnamon, and sugar until thick and creamy. Whip cream until stiff and fold into cinnamon cream. Rinse out 4 individual molds with cold water, fill with the cream, and place in the freezer for at least 2 hours.

For the red wine pears: Combine red wine, sugar, cinnamon stick, cloves and nutmeg, and bring to a boil. In the meantime, peel pears without removing the stems and place them in the red wine liquid. Cook gently over low heat for

15–20 minutes. (If the pears are not completely covered by the liquid, you will have to rotate or turn them occasionally.) Let pears cool and when completely cooled, refrigerate in the liquid.

Take molds from the freezer, let thaw slightly or, if desired, place briefly in hot water and reverse parfaits onto 4 plates. Arrange cold pears beside the parfaits and drizzle with a little of the liquid.

☞ You can also make the parfaits in a small terrine or loaf pan; after freezing, reverse out the pan and cut into slices.

Pear and Cheese Soufflé

2 tbs butter, 1 tbs flour, 7 oz milk, 7 oz heavy cream, 7 tbs sweet grapes,
1 large pear, 3½ tbs sliced almonds, 3 eggs, 7 tbs freshly grated
Emmenthaler cheese, 7 tbs chopped Roquefort cheese (or any blue cheese)
Plus: Butter for the casserole dish

In a saucepan, heat butter until foamy and stir in flour. While stirring constantly, add milk and cream and reduce for about 10 minutes until thick and creamy. Remove from heat and let sauce cool. In the meantime, remove stems from grapes and rinse. Peel pear, cut into quarters, core, and cut into small pieces. Butter a casserole dish, sprinkle the bottom with sliced almonds, and distribute fruit on top. Separate eggs and mix cooled sauce with egg yolks, Emmenthaler, and Roquefort. Beat egg whites until stiff and fold in. Spoon sauce onto fruit. Bake in an oven preheated to 350°F for 30–35 minutes until golden. Serve immediately.

☞ Serve with a fresh baguette and a small glass of chilled dessert wine.
☞ You can also prepare this extravagant dessert in individual casserole dishes.

Pear Mascarpone Cream

1 large pear, 1 tsp sugar, Juice of ½ lemon
For the cream: 7 tbs sugar, 3 egg yolks, 1 cup mascarpone cheese,
3½ tbs pear brandy, 1 tbs powdered sugar

Peel pear, cut into quarters, core, and cut into thin slices. In a saucepan, combine 7 oz water, sugar and lemon juice, and bring to a boil. Add pear slices and simmer over low heat for 5 minutes. Remove pears and transfer to a plate to cool. For the cream: Beat sugar and egg yolks until foamy. Stir in mascarpone and brandy.

In glass bowls, alternate layers of pear slices and mascarpone cream, finishing with a layer of cream. Dust with a thick coating of powdered sugar. Cover and refrigerate for about 1 hour.

☞ Just before serving, insert 2 ladyfingers in each bowl.

Baked Pear Fans with Prosecco Cream

8 small pear halves (canned), 3 tbs pear brandy, 2 tbs sugar,
2 eggs, ⅔ cup Prosecco (or sparkling wine),
1 tsp vanilla extract, 1 tbs powdered sugar

Drain pear halves briefly. Cut each pear half into thin slices lengthwise, leaving the slices attached at the stem end. On each of 4 soup plates, arrange 2 pear halves spread out into a fan shape. Combine sugar and brandy and drizzle onto pears.

Separate eggs and beat egg whites until stiff. In a heat-resistant bowl, beat egg yolks, Prosecco, and vanilla over a hot double boiler for 5 minutes until thick and creamy. Then beat cream over a cold double boiler and fold in egg whites.

Spoon Prosecco cream over the marinated pear fans and dust with powdered sugar. Bake in an oven preheated to 350°F for 8–10 minutes.

 If you prefer to make this dessert using fresh pears, first poach the pears in water with a little sugar.

Bartlett Cream with Pear Wedges

*1 cup heavy cream, 1 pkg powdered gelatin, 1 cup milk,
3 egg yolks, ¼ cup sugar, 4 tbs pear brandy
For garnish: ½ pear (Bartlett or Bosc), 1 tbs pear brandy*

Whip cream until stiff and refrigerate until you need it. Soften gelatin in cold water. Bring milk to a boil. In a heat-resistant bowl, beat egg yolks and sugar and continue beating as you add the milk. Beat this mixture over a hot double boiler until it takes on a thick and creamy consistency. Squeeze out gelatin, add to mixture, and continue stirring until gelatin has completely dissolved. Flavor cream with brandy and then beat over a cold double boiler. Fold in whipped cream and transfer mixture to individual bowls. Cover and refrigerate for at least 2 hours.

For the garnish: Just before serving, peel pears, core, and cut into thin wedges. Arrange decoratively on the bowls of cream and drizzle with brandy. Flambé if desired.

Bartlett Pear Soufflé

5 tsp sugar, ½ vanilla bean, 1 ripe pear (Bartlett),
4 tsp pear brandy, 1 egg, ½ tsp powdered sugar
Plus: 1 tbs melted butter for the individual ramekins

In a saucepan, combine 1 cup water and 2 tsp sugar and bring to a boil. Slit open vanilla bean and add. Peel pear, cut into quarters, core, and cut up coarsely. Add to the saucepan and simmer for about 10 minutes.

Remove pear and drain well. In a bowl, purée pear with brandy and remaining sugar. Separate egg. Beat egg yolk until thick and creamy and stir into pear purée. Cover bowl with plastic wrap and refrigerate for 30 minutes. Beat egg white with powdered sugar until stiff and, using a wooden spoon, thoroughly fold into the pear cream.

Brush 4 individual ovenproof ramekins (2- to 2½-inch diameters) with butter all the way to the rims. Fill with pear cream to within ⅜ inch of the top. Bake in an oven preheated to 400°F for 8–9 minutes. Serve immediately.

☞ You can also make this same recipe using apples and Calvados.

Pear Apple Casserole with Honey

4 two-day-old bread rolls, 3 eggs, 2 cups milk,
1 tsp vanilla extract, 3 tbs honey, 1 lb apples, 1 lb pears,
7 tbs apricot jam, Juice of 1 lemon, 7 tbs slivered almonds,
1 pinch mace, ¼ tsp cinnamon, 1 pinch cloves
Plus: Butter for the casserole dish,
2–3 tbs sugar and ½ tsp cinnamon for topping

Cut bread rolls into slices ¼-inch thick and place in a bowl. Beat eggs, milk, vanilla and honey, and pour over bread roll slices. Peel apples and pears, cut into quarters, core, and cut into wedges. Slightly heat apricot jam, stir in lemon juice, and mix with fruit.

Butter a large casserole dish and line the bottom and sides with ⅔ of the softened bread slices. Combine fruit mixture, slivered almonds, mace, cinnamon and cloves, and pour into the center of the casserole dish. Top with remaining bread slices. Bake in an oven preheated to 350°F for up to 50 minutes. Remove and sprinkle liberally with a mixture of sugar and cinnamon. Serve in the casserole dish.

☞ When I was growing up, we often had this casserole as a main dish.

Baked Cranberry Pears

2 pears, Juice of ½ lemon, 1 cup white wine, 1 tbs sugar, 2 whole cloves,
4 tbs cranberry sauce, 2 egg whites, ½ tsp vanilla extract

Peel pears, cut in half, and remove a liberal amount of the core. In a saucepan, combine lemon juice, white wine, sugar and cloves, and bring to a boil and add pear halves. Gently simmer over low heat for 5 minutes. Remove pears, drain briefly, fill each with 1 tbs cranberry sauce, and place in a casserole dish. Pour pear liquid all around.

Beat egg whites with vanilla until stiff and spread onto pear halves. Preheat oven to 400°F, set to broil, and heat for 5 minutes. Serve immediately.

☞ Ideal as a fruity accompaniment to a cheese platter.

Chocolate Fruit Fondue

For dipping: 2 apples, 2 pears, 2 bananas,
1 cup strawberries, 8–12 ladyfingers (optional)
For the fondue: ⅔ lb milk chocolate (about 10½ oz), 7 oz heavy cream

Peel apples and pears, cut into quarters, core, and cut into bite-sized morsels. Peel bananas and slice. Remove stems from strawberries, rinse, and pat dry with paper towels. Arrange all the dipping ingredients on separate plates.

For the fondue: Break up chocolate, place in a heat-resistant bowl with cream, and melt carefully over a hot double boiler. Pour chocolate mixture into 4 small bowls and arrange on the table with one for each guest. Alternately dip prepared ingredients into the chocolate and enjoy.

☞ You can also use a special ceramic chocolate fondue pot with an integrated stand for a tea light. But this isn't absolutely necessary. Besides, it's easier to avoid splattering when each guest can dip into their own individual bowl.

Fruit Salad with Cinnamon Cream

7 oz purple and white grapes, 1 orange, 1 apple, 1 pear, 1 banana,
2 tbs orange liqueur, 3½ tbs mixed fruit juice, 7 oz heavy cream,
1 tbs sugar, 1 large pinch cinnamon

Rinse grapes, remove stems, and cut larger ones in half, removing seeds as necessary. Peel orange so that the white outer membrane is also removed, and use a small, sharp knife to cut segments from between the inner membranes.

Peel apple and pear, cut into quarters, core, and cut into small slices. Peel banana and slice. In a bowl, lightly toss prepared fruits with orange liqueur and fruit juice. Whip cream with sugar and cinnamon until stiff. Transfer fruit salad to individual bowls and garnish with cinnamon cream.

☞ Depending on the season and your preference, you can also make fruit salads from a single type of fruit. If you want, sprinkle the cinnamon cream with toasted, sliced almonds.

JAMS AND JELLIES

Pear Jam with Plums

1 lb plums, 2¼ lb pears, 3 tbs pear brandy, 7 cups sugar,
1 pkg liquid fruit pectin (about 3 oz)

Rinse plums, cut in half, and remove pits. Peel pears, cut into quarters, core, and cut up coarsely. In a blender, finely purée plums and pears with 2 tbs brandy.

In a saucepan, combine purée and sugar and bring to a full rolling boil, stirring constantly. Stir in pectin. Return to full rolling boil. Boil 1 minute, stirring constantly. Remove from heat and skim with metal spoon. Cool 5 minutes, skim again. Pour immediately into hot, sterilized jelly jars. Rinse out jar lids with remaining brandy (pour from lid to lid) and screw tightly onto the jars.

☞ You can also use Chinese plum wine or plum brandy in place of the pear brandy.

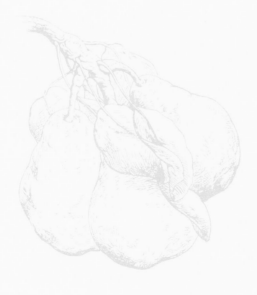

Pear Jam with Dates

1 lb fresh dates, 1 lb pears, 3 tbs Madeira, Juice of ½ lemon,
5 cups sugar, 1 pkg powdered fruit pectin (about 1¾ oz)

With a small, pointed knife, carefully peel dates and remove pits. Peel pears, cut into quarters, core, and cut into small pieces. In a blender, finely purée dates and pears with Madeira and lemon juice.

In a saucepan, combine fruit mixture and pectin and bring to a boil. Add sugar and bring back to full rolling boil. Boil 1 minute. Remove from heat and skim with metal spoon. Cool 5 minutes, skim again. Pour immediately into hot, sterilized jelly jars and seal tightly.

☞ Take 8–10 of the freshly peeled dates and replace the pits with almonds. Mix these into the finished jam—makes a great practical joke at breakfast!

Apple Jam with Blackberries

2¼ lb blackberries, 1 lb tart apples, Juice and grated peel of ½ lemon,
3½ tbs sherry, 7 cups sugar, 1 pkg liquid fruit pectin (about 3 oz)

Sort blackberries, rinse, and pat dry with paper towels. Peel apples, cut into quarters, core, and cut into small, uniform pieces. In a bowl, combine blackberries, apple pieces, lemon juice, lemon peel, and sherry. Cover with plastic wrap and let stand for 30 minutes.

In a saucepan, combine fruit mixture and sugar and bring to a full rolling boil, stirring constantly. Stir in pectin. Return to full rolling boil. Boil 1 minute, stirring constantly. Remove from heat and skim with metal spoon. Cool 5 minutes, skim again. Pour immediately into hot, sterilized jelly jars and seal tightly.

☞ You can also use currants or gooseberries in place of the blackberries.

Pumpkin Jam with Apples

*2¼ lb pumpkin flesh, 1 lb apples, Juice of 1 lemon, 7 cups sugar,
1 pkg liquid fruit pectin (about 3 oz), 2 tbs apple schnapps*

Peel pumpkin, remove fibers and seeds, and cut flesh into very small pieces. Peel apples, cut into quarters, core, and cut into same size pieces as the pumpkin. In a blender, finely purée pumpkin and apples with lemon juice. In a saucepan, combine purée and sugar and bring to a full rolling boil, stirring constantly. Stir in pectin. Return to full rolling boil. Boil 1 minute, stirring constantly. Remove from heat and skim with metal spoon. Cool 5 minutes, skim again. Pour immediately into hot, sterilized jelly jars. Rinse out jar lids with apple schnapps (pour from lid to lid) and screw tightly onto the jars.

Apple Jam with Raisins

*2¼ lb apples, Juice of 1 lemon, 7 tbs raisins, ½ cup cider (apple wine),
1 pkg powdered fruit pectin (about 1¾ oz), 5 cups sugar*

Peel apples, cut into quarters, core, and dice finely. In a saucepan, combine apples, lemon juice, raisins, pectin and cider, and bring to a boil. Add sugar and bring back to full rolling boil. Boil 1 minute. Remove from heat and skim with metal spoon. Cool 5 minutes, skim again. Pour immediately into hot, sterilized jelly jars and seal tightly.

Raspberry Jam with Apples

3⅓ cups raspberries, 3⅓ cups apples, Juice of 1 lemon, 7 cups sugar,
1 pkg liquid fruit pectin (about 3 oz), 3½ tbs raspberry liqueur

Sort raspberries, rinse, and drain. Peel apples, cut into quarters, core, and cut into small pieces. In a blender, finely purée apples with lemon juice. In a saucepan, combine apple purée, sugar and raspberries, and bring to a full rolling boil, stirring constantly. Stir in pectin. Return to full rolling boil. Boil 1 minute, stirring constantly. Remove from heat and skim with metal spoon. Cool 5 minutes, skim again. Pour immediately into hot, sterilized jelly jars. Rinse out jar lids with raspberry liqueur (pour from lid to lid) and screw tightly onto the jars.

Apple Jelly

3⅓ lb apples, 1 cup cider (apple wine), Juice of 1 lemon, 2¼ lb sugar

Peel apples, core, and cut up coarsely. Combine apples, cider, and lemon juice and bring to a boil. Simmer for about 20 minutes until tender. Strain through a sieve lined with cheesecloth. Weight apple sauce with a plate so the juice can escape with only a little pressure.

For the jelly: Measure out 1 qt apple juice, combine with sugar, and bring to a boil. Boil uncovered for 2 minutes. Pour immediately into hot, sterilized jelly jars and seal tightly.

☞ Apples do not require a gelling agent because the fruit's own pectin is enough to make it gel. However, you can use pectin just to be on the safe side.
☞ Drizzle jar lids with orange liqueur to give the jelly a slight fragrance.

Apple Strawberry Jelly

3⅓ cups apple juice, 1 cup strawberry juice,
1 pkg powdered fruit pectin (about 1¾ oz), 5 cups sugar

In a saucepan, combine apple juice, strawberry juice and pectin, and bring to a boil. Add sugar and bring back to full rolling boil. Boil 1 minute. Remove from heat and skim with metal spoon. Cool 5 minutes, skim again. Pour immediately into hot, sterilized jelly jars and seal tightly.

Elderberry Jelly with Apple Fragrance

4 cups elderberry juice, ½ cup apple juice,
1 pkg powdered fruit pectin (about 1¾ oz), 5 cups sugar

In a saucepan, combine elderberry juice, apple juice and pectin, and bring to a boil. Add sugar and bring back to full rolling boil. Boil 1 minute. Remove from heat and skim with metal spoon. Cool 5 minutes, skim again. Pour immediately into hot, sterilized jelly jars and seal tightly.

☞ Spread elderberry jelly on fresh buttered rolls and serve with fresh apple pieces wrapped in slices of cooked ham.

DIPS, SAUCES, AND CHUTNEYS

Cheese Horseradish Cream

*7 tbs Grana Padano or Sbrinz cheese (or any hard grating cheese such
as Parmesan), ½ cup full-fat cream cheese, 1 apple,
1 tbs freshly grated horseradish, Salt, Freshly ground black pepper,
⅔ cup heavy cream, Hungarian sweet paprika*

Grate cheese finely and mix with cream cheese. Peel apple, core, and grate into
cheese mixture. Season with horseradish, salt, and pepper. Whip cream until stiff
and fold in. Pour cream into 4 individual bowls and dust with paprika.

☞ Goes with various types of bread, but can also serve as a dip for Italian and
sourdough breadsticks.

Gorgonzola Pear Dip

*7 oz Gorgonzola cheese, 7 oz heavy cream, 1 pear,
Salt, Freshly ground black pepper, 1 tsp green peppercorns*

In a bowl, mash Gorgonzola with a fork while stirring in half the cream. Peel
pear, core, and grate into cheese mixture using a kitchen grater. Season with salt
and pepper. Whip remaining cream until stiff and fold into cheese cream. Pour
dip into individual bowls and garnish with green peppercorns.

Stilton Cream with Pear Balls

*⅔ lb Stilton cheese (about 10½ oz; English blue cheese),
7 oz ricotta, ½ bunch chives, 1 pear*

Chop Stilton. Beat Stilton and ricotta until creamy. Place this cream in the center of 4 plates. Rinse chives, pat dry, chop, and sprinkle over the top. Peel pear, cut in half lengthwise, core, and, using a melon baller, make into little balls. Arrange these balls around the cheese cream.

☞ Simmer pear balls in 7 tbs dry red wine for 5 minutes and then spoon them around the cheese cream.

Barolo Pears with Gorgonzola Cream

*4 small pears, 2 cups Barolo (Italian red wine), 7 oz Gorgonzola cheese,
3½ tbs softened butter, 2 tbs chopped pistachios or walnuts*

Peel pears, cut in half lengthwise, and remove a liberal amount of the core or hollow out. In a saucepan, bring Barolo to a boil. Add pear halves and cook gently over low heat for 5-8 minutes.

In the meantime, chop Gorgonzola. Beat Gorgonzola and butter until creamy. Drain pear halves briefly and arrange 2 pear halves on each of 4 plates with the hollow sides up. Place cheese cream in a pastry bag and pipe decoratively into the pear halves. Garnish with pistachios or walnuts.

Fruity Banana Sauce

1 small ripe banana, Juice of ½ orange, 1 tart apple,
2 tbs mango chutney (prepared product), 7 oz sour cream,
1 pinch sugar, Salt, Freshly ground black pepper, ¼ tsp curry
For dipping: 1 pkg shrimp chips (krupuk, from
Asian markets and some supermarkets)

Peel banana and, in a bowl, mash with a fork. Drizzle with orange juice. Peel apple, core, and grate finely into the bowl. Stir in mango chutney and sour cream. Season liberally with sugar, salt, pepper, and curry. Pour sauce into 4 individual bowls and dust with curry. Serve as a dip with krupuk.

☞ You can also serve tortilla chips. Or heat tortillas, spread sauce over the entire surface, roll up, and serve as wraps.

Nut Paste with Apples and Chile Pepper

4 green onions, 2 cloves garlic, 1 red chile pepper, 3½ tbs pine nuts,
3½ tbs cashews, 3½ tbs walnuts, 1 apple, 2 tbs lemon juice,
3½ tbs olive oil, Salt, Freshly ground black pepper

Clean green onions and dice finely. Peel garlic. Remove stem, seeds, and interiors from chile pepper. Mince garlic and chile pepper. Finely chop pine nuts, cashews, and walnuts and toast in a hot, ungreased pan while stirring until they give off an aroma. Transfer to a plate.

Peel apple, cut into quarters, core, and dice finely. Drizzle with lemon juice. In a pan, heat 2 tbs olive oil and briefly braise green onions, garlic, and chile pepper. Transfer pan contents to a blender, add remaining olive oil, and purée. Stir in apple pieces and nuts. Season with salt and pepper.

☞ Pour paste into a small bowl and garnish with fresh apple wedges and walnut halves.

Warm Apple-Based Sauce

2 apples (e.g., Cox's Orange Pippin),
Grated peel and juice of 1 lemon, 3½ tbs chicken stock,
1 tbs Calvados (apple brandy), 7 tbs heavy cream,
Salt, Freshly ground black pepper

Peel apples, cut into quarters, core, and dice finely. In a small saucepan, combine apples, lemon peel and lemon juice, and simmer gently for about 15 minutes. Add chicken stock, Calvados, and cream. As soon as mixture starts to boil, purée sauce with a hand blender until smooth. Season with salt and pepper and serve hot or warm.

☞ Excellent with grilled dishes or cooked meat.

Apple Sauerkraut Dip

2 cups vegetable stock, 7 tbs millet, 1 red bell pepper, 1 small onion,
½ bunch chives, 1 apple, 7 tbs sauerkraut (ready-to-serve),
3 tbs olive oil, Salt, Freshly ground black pepper

Bring vegetable stock to a boil. Sprinkle in millet and boil for 10 minutes while stirring repeatedly. Remove from heat and let millet stand for 20 minutes.

In the meantime, cut bell pepper in half, remove seeds and interiors, and dice finely. Peel onion and dice finely. Rinse chives, pat dry, and chop. Peel apple, cut into quarters, core, and grate finely. Chop sauerkraut somewhat finer. In a bowl, lightly toss millet, bell pepper, onion, chives, apple, sauerkraut, and olive oil. Season with salt and pepper.

☞ This nutritious dip is especially delicious with whole-wheat bread. You can also garnish it with freshly grated apple sprinkled over the top.

Apple Chutney with Raisins

2¼ lb apples (e.g., McIntosh), 7 oz onions, 1 cup raisins,
7 oz brown rock sugar, 1 tbs mustard seeds, Salt, Cayenne pepper,
3½ tbs vinegar concentrate (25%), 7 oz water,
Freshly ground white pepper

Peel apples, cut into quarters, core, and cut crosswise into thin slices. Peel onions and cut into rings.

In a large saucepan, combine apple slices, onion rings, raisins, rock sugar, mustard seeds, salt, cayenne, vinegar concentrate, and water. Bring to a boil and then simmer over low heat for 30–40 minutes, stirring occasionally, until almost all the liquid has boiled away. Season chutney with pepper, pour immediately into hot, sterilized jelly jars, and seal tightly.

Apple Pear Chutney

1 onion, 1 cucumber, 1 lb apples, 1 lb pears, 3½ tbs pear brandy,
3 tbs vegetable oil, ¼ tsp curry, 1 cup brown sugar, ⅔ cup fruit vinegar,
1 tsp salt, 1 tsp pickled green peppercorns, 1 pinch cayenne pepper

Peel and mince onion. Peel cucumber, cut in half lengthwise, scrape out seeds with a spoon, and cut crosswise into thin slices. Peel apples and pears, cut into quarters, core, and cut into thin wedges. Drizzle with brandy.

In a large saucepan, heat vegetable oil and braise minced onion until translucent. Then stir in cucumber, apple and pear pieces, and braise for 2 minutes. Add curry, cane sugar, fruit vinegar, salt, peppercorns, and cayenne. As soon as the mixture starts to boil, reduce heat and simmer gently over low heat for about 40 minutes, stirring repeatedly. Then remove from heat, pour immediately into hot, sterilized jelly jars, seal tightly, and store in a cool place.

☞ Individual bowls of warm Apple Pear Chutney can also be served immediately as a side with foil-wrapped baked potatoes.

Tomato Chutney with Fruit

1 onion, 1 lb tomatoes, 1 cup apricots, 1 cup apples,
2 tbs vegetable oil, 1 cup brown sugar, 1 cup white wine vinegar,
1 tsp salt, 5 black peppercorns

Peel and mince onion. Blanch tomatoes, rinse under cold water, remove seeds and cores, and dice finely. Pour hot water over apricots, peel, remove pits, and cut into same size pieces as tomatoes. Peel apples, cut into quarters, core, and dice finely.

In a saucepan, heat vegetable oil and braise minced onion until translucent. Add tomatoes, apricots and apples, and braise for 2 minutes. Then stir in sugar, vinegar, salt, and peppercorns. As soon as the mixture starts to boil, reduce heat and simmer gently for about 30 minutes, stirring repeatedly. Remove from heat, pour immediately into hot, sterilized jelly jars, and seal tightly.

☞ This chutney is delicious hot, warm, and cold, as a spread on flatbread or on a baguette. It's ideal for picnics or as a topping for grilled steak.

Carrot Apple Chutney with Lemon

1 small red chile pepper, ¾ inch fresh ginger (about a thumb-sized piece),
1 lemon, 7 tbs fresh dates, 1 cup carrots, 1 lb apples,
1 cup brown sugar, 1 cup white wine vinegar, ½ tsp salt, ½ tsp turmeric

Cut chile pepper in half lengthwise, remove stem, seeds and interior, and dice finely. Peel ginger and mince. Rinse lemon under hot water, pat dry, and use a zester to grate extremely fine strips from the peel. Remove the white membrane from the lemon and dice fruit finely, removing any seeds.

Carefully peel dates, remove pits, and chop finely. Peel carrots and apples. Cut apples into quarters, core, and finely dice both carrots and apples.

In a saucepan, melt sugar. Stir in vinegar, salt, and turmeric. Gradually add chile pepper, ginger, lemon peel, diced lemon, dates, carrots, and apples. As soon as the mixture starts to boil, reduce heat and simmer gently over low heat for 40 minutes, stirring repeatedly, until you have a runny mixture. Remove from heat, pour immediately into hot, sterilized jelly jars, and seal tightly.

☞ Delicious as a dip with grilled meat or vegetables. But it's also highly recommended as a tangy chutney for wok dishes.

LIST OF RECIPES

Hearty Entrées and Sides

Fruity Cakes and Pastries

Desserts and Treats

Abbreviations

lb = pound
oz = ounce
pkg = package
qt = quart
tbs = tablespoon
tsp = teaspoon